Spanish-English/English-Spanish
Pocket Legal Dictionary

Diccionario Jurídico de Bolsillo
Español-Inglés/Inglés-Español

Spanish-English/English-Spanish
Pocket Legal Dictionary

Diccionario Jurídico de Bolsillo
Español-Inglés/Inglés-Español

James Nolan

HIPPOCRENE BOOKS, INC.
New York

Series Editor: Lynn Visson
Series Consultant: James Nolan

For information, address:
  HIPPOCRENE BOOKS, INC.
  171 Madison Ave.
  New York, NY 10016
  www.hippocrenebooks.com

Library of Congress Cataloging-in-Publication Data

Nolan, James, 1946–
  Spanish-English/English-Spanish pocket legal
  dictionary = Diccionario juridico de bolsillo espanolingles/
  ingles-espanol / James Nolan.
       p. cm.
  ISBN-13: 978-0-7818-1214-6 (alk. paper)
  ISBN-10: 0-7818-1214-3 (alk. paper)
    1. Law—Dictionaries. 2. Law—Dictionaries—
  Spanish. 3. English language—Dictionaries—Spanish.
  4. Spanish language—Dictionaries—English. I. Title.
  II. Title: Diccionario juridico de bolsillo espanol-ingles/
  ingles-espanol.
  K52.S6N65 2008
  340.03—dc22

                                              2008015016

Contents

Foreword

This pocket dictionary is designed to help those individuals who need to communicate in real-life situations where it is vital to quickly find an English or Spanish legal term or phrase. The organization of the book is therefore more practical than analytical: entries are not listed strictly according to the conventions of lexicography or grammar, nouns are listed in the plural if such usage is common usage, phrases that function as verbs or nouns are listed as such, etc. Without attempting to be exhaustive, we have sought to include most of the terms or concepts relevant to everyday legal situations and currently in use. The reader should be aware that legal terms can be specific to a culture and exact equivalents in another language do not always exist. Some legal topics have developed more specialized terminology, while others are of a more general character and are addressed in the dictionary's initial sections on general and procedural terms.

Prefacio

Este diccionario de bolsillo está dirigido a quienes cotidianamente necesitan recurrir a términos o frases legales en español o inglés. Su organización responde más a necesidades prácticas, antes que analíticas: el listado de términos no responde estrictamente a un orden lexicográfico o gramatical, se incluye el plural de los sustantivos cuando son de uso común, así como frases con función verbal o sustantiva. El lector debe tener en cuenta que el lenguaje jurídico es propio de cada cultura y que no siempre existen equivalencias exactas en otra lengua. Algunos temas jurídicos han desarrollado una terminología más especializada, mientras que otros son más genéricos. Éstos últimos son abordados en la primera sección del diccionario sobre Términos Generales y Procesales.

NOTES ON PRONUNCIATION AND GENDER

How to Pronounce Spanish

Most of the sounds of Spanish are close enough to English sounds that you will be understood if you pronounce the word as if it were an English word, as long as you remember the following:

Vowels

English vowels can be pronounced in more than one way (as in "rule" and "put") but Spanish vowels always have only one sound:

a	like the *a* in fat
e	like the *e* in fed
i	like the *ee* in weed
o	like the *o* in cord
u	like the *u* in rule

Consonants (differing from English)

j	like the *ch* in Bach
ll	like the *y* in youth
g	before *a, o, u*, like the *g* in go
	before *e, i*, like the *ch* in Bach

h	always silent
ñ	like the *ny* in canyon
rr	*rolled*
z	like the *s* in soft

Stress

In Spanish the stress usually falls on the next-to-last syllable of a word. If another syllable is to be stressed, a written accent mark is used to show it.

Gender of nouns

Spanish nouns ending in -o are almost always masculine in gender (e.g. *el gato*). Those ending in -a are almost always feminine in gender (e.g. *la casa*). For all nouns, the gender is indicated in the Spanish-English section.

ABBREVIATIONS

Abbreviation	English	Spanish
adj	adjective	adjetivo
adv	adverb	adverbio
n	noun	sustantivo
nm	masculine noun	sustantivo masculine
nf	feminine noun	sustantivo femenino
v	verb	verbo

ESPAÑOL – INGLÉS
SPANISH – ENGLISH

TÉRMINOS GENERALES Y PROCESALES
GENERAL AND PROCEDURAL TERMS

a sabiendas *adv* knowingly
abandonar *v* abandon
abandono *nm* abandonment
abogado *nm* lawyer
abogado de la causa *nm* attorney of record
abogado del caso *nm* attorney of record
abrogar *v* abrogate
abusar *v* abuse
abuso *nm* abuse
abuso de confianza *nm* abuse of trust
abuso de poder *nm* abuse of power
acatar *v* comply with
acceso carnal *nm* sexual intercourse
acción judicial colectiva *nf* class action
acoso *nm* harassment
acta *nf* certificate, record
acta literal *nm* verbatim record
acta taquigráfica *nf* transcript, verbatim record
actas del juicio *nf* trial record
acto *nm* deed, act
acuerdo *nm* agreement
acusado *nm* accused
adicción *nm* addiction

Términos Generales y Procesales

adicto *nm* addict; *adj* addicted
administración *nf* administration
administración de casos *nf* caseflow management
administrador *nm* administrator
administrar *v* administer
administrativo *adj* administrative
admisión *nf* admission
aduanas *nf* customs
adulto *nm/adj* adult
adversidad *nf* hardship
advertir *v* warn
advertir oficialmente *v* serve notice, put on notice
afidávit *nm* affidavit
afirmar *v* affirm
agencia de cobranza *nf* collection agency
agotamiento de recursos *nm* exhaustion of remedies
agravio *nm* grievance, injury
agregar firma *v* affix signature
ajustador (de seguros) *nm* (insurance) adjuster
albacea testamentario *nm/nf* executor
alcohol *nm* alcohol
alcohólico *n/adj* alcoholic
alcoholismo *nm* alcoholism
alegación *nf* allegation
alegar *v* allege
alegato *nm* pleading, argument, allegation
alegato de apertura *nm* opening statement
alegatos finales *nm* closing argument
alentar *v* encourage
alguacil *nm* bailiff
alterado *adj* agitated, distraught

alterar *v* alter, modify
alterar fraudulentamente *v* tamper with
alterno *adj* alternate
amenaza *nf* threat
amenazar *v* threaten
amonestación *nf* admonition
amonestar *v* admonish
amparo *nm* constitutional appeal
analizar los hechos *v* examine the facts
anfetamina *nf* amphetamine
ánimo *nm* intention
anular *v* cancel, repeal, annul
apelación *nf* appeal
apelado *nm* appellee, respondent on appeal
apelante *nm* appellant
apelar *v* appeal
aplazamiento *(de un juicio o una audiencia)* *nm*
     continuance *(postponement of a trial or hearing)*
aptitud *nm* aptitude, eligibility
apto *adj* apt, eligible, qualified, competent
apto para dar testimonio *adj* competent to testify
apto para ir a juicio *adj* competent to stand trial
apurado *adj* hurried, rushed
apurarse *v* hurry, rush
apuro *nm* rush, trouble, predicament
argüir *v* argue
argumentar *v* argue
argumento *nm* argument
arma *nf* weapon
arreglo *nm* settlement, arrangement
artículo *nm* article

asesor legal *nm* attorney, counselor at law
asistencia *nf* attendance
asistencia judicial internacional *nf* international
    judicial assistance
asistente social *nm* caseworker
asistir *v* assist, facilitate
asunto *nm* affair, matter
atenuante *adj* extenuating, mitigating
atestiguar *v* testify, give evidence
atrasado *adj* delayed, late
atrasos *nm* arrears
audiencia *nf* hearing, trial
ausentismo escolar *nm* truancy
auténtico *adj* authentic, genuine
auto *nm* decree
averiguar *v* inquire, investigate
banda *nf* gang, mob
base razonable *nm* reasonable basis
bien mueble *nm* chattel, personal property
bono *nm* bond
borrachería *nf* drunkenness
borracho *adj* drunk; *nm* drunkard
búsqueda *nf* search
caducidad *nf* expiration
cantidad *nf* quantity, sum, amount
capaz *adj* competent, capable, qualified
capaz de someterse a juicio *adj* competent to
    stand trial
carga de la prueba *nf* burden of proof
caso *nm* case
cedente *nm* assignor

ceder *v* assign
ceñirse a *v* comply with
certificado de defunción *nm* death certificate
cesión *nm* assignment
cesionario *nm* assignee
circunvenir *v* circumvent
cita *nf* date, appointment
citación *nf* summons
citar a comparecer *v* summon
cláusula *nf* clause
coca *nf* coca
cocaína *nf* cocaine
cofirmante *nm* co-signer
coito *nm* sexual intercourse
colegio de abogados *nm* bar
comisión *nf* commission
comparecencia *nf* appearance
comparecer ante el tribunal *v* appear in court
compensación *nf* compensation, setoff
competencia *nf* jurisdiction
competencia en razón de la materia *nf* subject
     matter, jurisdiction
con perjuicio *adj/adv* with prejudice
conciliación *nf* conciliation
conducta *nf* conduct, behavior
conducta indecente *nf* lewd conduct
conducta lasciva *nf* lewd conduct
confidencial *adj* confidential
confirmación (de una decisión) *nf* affirmance *(of
     a decision)*
consentimiento *nm* consent

Términos Generales y Procesales

consentimiento válido *nm* informed consent
consentir *v* consent
conserje *nm* usher
considerar los hechos *v* examine the facts
consolidación de acciones *nf* consolidation of actions
constitución *nf* constitution
constitucional *adj* constitutional
cónsul *nm* consul
consulado *nm* consulate
consumidor *nm* consumer
contractual *adj* contractual
contrademanda *nf* counterclaim
contrademandar *v* counterclaim
contrainterrogatorio *nm* cross-examination
contrato *nm* contract
contumacia *nf* contempt of court
contusión cerebral *nf* brain contusion
convención *nf* convention
convenio *nm* agreement
corporal *adj* bodily, tangible
correo registrado *nm* certified mail
corroborado *adj* corroborated
corroborar *v* corroborate
corromper *v* corrupt
corrupción *nf* corruption
corrupto *adj* corrupt
cosa juzgada *nf* res judicata
costar *v* cost
costas judiciales *nf* court costs
costo *nm* cost
credibilidad *nf* credibility

General and Procedural Terms

creíble *adj* credible
crimen *nm* crime
culpa *nf* guilt, blame
culpabilidad *nf* culpability
curador *nm* conservator
curatela *nf* conservatorship
custodia *nf* custody
custodia de la prueba *nf* custody of evidence
dañino *adj* harmful
daño *nm* harm, injury
daños físicos *nm* bodily injury, bodily harm
daños líquidos y determinados *nm* liquidated damages
daños punitorios *nm* punitive damages
dar lugar a un pedimento *v* grant a motion
de acuerdo con la ley *adv* by operation of law
deber de cautela, deber de diligencia *nm* duty of care
declaración *nf* statement
declaración jurada *nf* deposition
declaración por escrito *nf* written statement, deposition
declarante *nm* declarant, witness, deponent
declarar *v* declare, testify, give evidence
decreto *nm* decree
defender *v* defend
defendido *nm* defendant
defensa *nf* defense
deficiencia mental *nf* mental deficiency
deliberado *adj* deliberate
deliberar *v* deliberate
delincuencia *nf* delinquency, crime
delincuente *adj/n* delinquent, criminal
delito *nm* offense, crime

delito civil *nm* tort
demanda *nf* complaint *(civil)*
demandado *nm* defendant
demandante *nm* plaintiff, complainant, claimant
demarcación *nf* district
demencia *nf* insanity, dementia
demente *adj* insane
demora *nf* delay
demorar *v* delay
denegar un pedimento *v* deny a motion
denegar una objeción *v* overrule an objection
denuncia *nf* complaint *(criminal)*
deponente *nm* deponent
deponer *v* depose
deposición *nf* deposition
depresión mental *nf* mental depression
derecho fundamental *nm* fundamental right
desacato *nm* contempt of court
desafiar *v* challenge
desafío *nm* challenge
descalificado *adj* disqualified
descalificar *v* disqualify
descuidar *v* neglect
descuido *nm* carelessness, neglect
desembolso *nm* disbursement
desestimación *nf* dismissal
desestimación con/sin pérdida de derecho *nf*
    dismissal with/without prejudice
desestimar *v* dismiss, reject
desistimiento *nm* discontinuance
determinación *nf* finding

determinación de hechos *nf* fact finding
devolver un caso a un tribunal *v* remand
dictamen *nm* ruling, expert opinion
difamación *nf* defamation
difunto *nm* decedent, deceased
diligencia *nf* procedure
diligenciamiento *nm* service *(of process)*
diligenciar *v* process, accomplish
disputar *v* argue, dispute
distinguir entre el bien y el mal *v* distinguish between
    right and wrong
distrito *nm* district
divulgación *nf* disclosure
divulgar *v* disclose
domicilio *nm* domicile
droga *nf* drug
drogar *v* drug
ebriedad *nm* drunkenness
ebrio *adj* inebriated, drunk; *nm* inebriate, drunk
edad *nf* age
ejecución *nf* execution
ejecución de sentencia *nf* enforcement of judgment
ejecutar *v* execute
elegible *adj* eligible, competent, qualified
embajada *nf* embassy
emitir *v* issue
enfermedad mental *nf* mental illness
engañar *v* deceive, trick
engaño *nm* deceit, deception, trickery
enmendar *v* amend
enmienda *nf* amendment

entablar querella *v* sue, file suit
entrega *nf* surrender
entregar *v* surrender, deliver, hand over
entregarse *v* surrender
equivocación *nf* mistake
error *nm* error, mistake
error substancial *nm* substantial error
escritura manuscrita *nf* handwriting
escucha subrepticia *nf* eavesdropping
esquizofrenia *nf* schizophrenia
estar en apuros *v* to be in trouble
estar en audiencia *v* to be in session
estar en sesión *v* to be in session
estatuto *nm* statute, bylaws
estenógrafo *nm* court reporter
estupefaciente *nm* narcotic
evaluación psiquiátrica *nf* psychiatric evaluation
evidencial *adj* evidentiary
examen clínico *nm* clinical examination
examen de ADN *nm* DNA test
examen del perito *nm* expert examination
examen del testigo *nm* examination of witness
examen directo *nm* direct examination
examen pericial *nm* expert examination
examinar *v* examine, question
excepción *nf* waiver, exception
exigir *v* demand
expediente del caso, expediente de la causa *nm*
    case file
expedir *v* issue
expirar *v* expire

exposición *nf* argument, account
expropiación *nf* condemnation *(of property)*
extracto *nm* extract, excerpt, abstract *(summary)*
extranjero *adj* foreign, alien; *nm* foreigner, alien
fallar *v* adjudicate, judge, rule
fallecido *nm* decedent
fallo *nm* ruling, judgment, arbitral award
fallo por incumplimiento *nm* default judgment
fallo probatorio *nm* evidentiary ruling
fallo sumario *nm* summary judgment
falsificar *v* falsify, tamper with
falta de jurisdicción *nf* lack of jurisdiction
fecha *nf* date
fecha de juicio *nf* trial date
fechoría *nf* malfeasance, wrongdoing
fedatario *nm* notary public
fidedigno *adj* reliable, trustworthy
fideicomisario *nm* trustee
fideicomiso *nm* trust
fiduciario *nm/adj* fiduciary
firma *nf* signature
firmar *v* sign
fiscal *nm* prosecutor
fiscal de distrito *nm* district attorney
foráneo *nm/adj* alien
forense *adj* forensic
fundamento *nm* ground, foundation
garantías procesales *nf* due process
genuino *adj* authentic, genuine
goce de derechos *nm* enjoyment of rights
haber patrimonial *nm* net worth

hashish *nm* hashish
heredar *v* inherit
heredero *nm* heir
herencia *nf* inheritance
herida *nf* wound
hogar de ancianos *nm* nursing home
homicidio culposo *nm* manslaughter
honorarios de abogado *nm* attorney's fees
idoneidad *nf* suitability, eligibility
idóneo *adj* suited, eligible, competent, qualified
igualdad de acuerdo con la ley *nf* equality under
    the law
ilegal *adj* illegal, unlawful
ilícito *adj* illegal, unlawful, illicit
impedido *adj* disqualified
impugnación del jurado *nf* jury challenge
impugnar *v* impeach, challenge
incapacidad mental *nf* mental incapacity
incitar *v* incite
inconducta *nf* misconduct
inconstitucional *adj* unconstitutional
incumplimiento *nm* breach, non-compliance
incumplimiento del deber *nm* breach of duty
incumplir *v* breach
indagatoria *nf* inquest
indemnización *nm* compensation, compensatory
    damages
indemnización de daños y perjuicios *nf* damages
inducir *v* induce
información y consentimiento *nm* informed consent
informe indagatorio *nm* record of investigation

informe médico *nm* medical report
informe sobre los sucesos *nm* incident report
infracción *nf* offense, violation
ingreso *nm* income, entry
ingreso disponible *nm* disposable income
ingreso ilegal *nm* illegal entry
inhabilitado *adj* disqualified
inhabilitar *v* disqualify
inmigración *nf* immigration
inmigrante *nm* immigrant
inmoral *adj* immoral
inmunidad limitada *nf* qualified immunity
instigar *v* instigate, incite
intentar querella *v* sue, bring suit
internar *v* commit *(confine)*
interpretación *nf* interpretation
interpretar *v* interpret
intérprete *nm* interpreter
interrogar *v* interrogate, question
interrogatorio directo *nm* direct examination
intestado *adj* intestate
intimidar *v* intimidate
intoxicación *nf* intoxication
investigación *nf* investigation, inquiry
investigación de hechos *nf* fact finding
investigar *v* investigate
involucrado *adj* involved, implicated
juez *nm* judge
juez auxiliar *nm* magistrate judge
juez magistrado *nm* magistrate judge
juez que preside *nm* presiding judge

General and Procedural Terms

juicio *nm* trial
juicio ante un juez *nm* bench trial, court trial
juicio colectivo *nm* class action
juicio nulo *nm* mistrial
jurado *nm* jury, juror; *adj* sworn
jurado indagatorio *nm* inquest jury
juramentar *v* swear an oath
juramento *nm* oath
jurar *v* swear
jurisdicción *nf* jurisdiction
jurisdicción sobre la persona *nf* personal jurisdiction
jurisdicción territorial *nf* territorial jurisdiction
jurisprudencia *nf* case-law
juzgado *nm* court, justice court
juzgar *v* judge, try
legal *adj* legal, lawful
legalización *nf* legalization
legislación *nf* legislation, statute
lesión *nf* injury, wound
lesión cerebral *nf* brain damage
lesión laboral *nf* work-related injury
lesiones *nf* bodily injury, bodily harm
letra *nf* handwriting
letrado *nm* counsel, attorney, counselor-at-law
levantar (actas) *v* draw up *(records)*
levantar (sesión) *v* adjourn *(meeting)*
ley *nf* law
ley escrita *nf* statute
libro *nm* book, volume, ledger
libro judicial *nm* docket
licenciado *nm* attorney, counselor

límite jurisdiccional *nm* jurisdictional limit
liquidador de seguros *nm* insurance adjuster
lista de casos *nm* docket
litigante *nm* litigant
litigar *v* litigate
litigio *nm* lawsuit, litigation, dispute
loco *adj* mad, insane
locura *nf* insanity, madness
mala fe *nf* bad faith
mandato *nm* power of attorney
mara *nf* gang
marihuana *nf* marijuana, cannabis, hemp
mediación *nf* mediation
mediador *nm* mediator
mediar *v* mediate
menor de edad *adj/nm* juvenile, minor
metanfetamina *nf* methamphetamine
miembro del jurado *nm* juror
monto *nm* amount, sum
moral *adj* moral
moralidad *nf* morality
motivo *nm* reason, ground, basis, motive
motivo para ordenar juicio nuevo *nm* grounds
    for re-trial
motivo razonable *nm* reasonable basis
móvil *nm* motive
muerte por negligencia *nf* wrongful death
multa *nf* fine
multar *v* fine
nacionalidad *nf* nationality
narcótico *nm* narcotic

negligencia *nf* negligence
negligencia grave *nf* gross negligence
negligente *adj* negligent
negligentemente *adv* negligently
notarial *adj* notarial
notario público *nm* civil-law notary
notificación de actos procesales *nf* service of process
notificar *v* notify, give notice
notificar *(actos procesales)* *v* serve, deliver *(process)*
notificar oficialmente *v* serve notice, put on notice
nueva vista de un caso *nf* new trial of a case
nuevo juicio *nm* re-trial
nulo e írrito *adj* null and void
obedecer *v* obey
objeción *nf* objection
obligatorio *adj* mandatory
obscenidad *nf* obscenity
obstáculo *nm* bar, obstacle
ocultar *v* conceal
orden *nf* order
orden de comparecencia *nf* summons
orden de protección *nm* protective order
orden judicial *nm* injunction, judicial order
ordenanza *(ley municipal)* *nf* ordinance *(municipal law)*
ordenar *v* order
pagos en mora *nm* arrears
pandilla *nf* gang, mob
panel de jueces *nm* panel of judges
parte *nf* party
partido *nm* district
pasaporte *nm* passport

patrimonio *nm* inheritance, net worth
pedimento *nm* motion
peligro inminente *nm* imminent danger
pena *nf* sentence, penalty, sanction
penal *adj* penal, criminal
penalidad *nf* penalty, sanction
pericia *nf* expertise
período de gracia *nm* grace period
perito *nm* expert, expert witness
perjudicial *adj* prejudicial
perjuicio *nm* harm, injury
permiso *nm* permit, permission
persona *nf* person
persona perjudicada *nf* injured party, aggrieved party
pesquisa *nf* investigation
petición *nf* petition, application, motion
plazo *nm* period, term
pleito *nm* quarrel, dispute, lawsuit
poder *nm* power, power of attorney
policía *nf* police department; *nm* police officer,
    policeman
por ministerio de ley *adv* by operation of law
por su cuenta y riesgo *adv* at your own risk
portador *nm* bearer
postergar *v* postpone
precedentes judiciales *nm* case law
pregunta sugestiva *nf* leading question
presenciar *v* witness, observe, perceive
presidir *v* preside, preside over
prestar juramento *v* swear, take an oath
presunción *nf* presumption

presunción absoluta *nf* irrebuttable presumption
prevenir oficialmente *v* serve notice, put on notice
previsible *adj* foreseeable
privación *nf* hardship
probar *v* prove
probatorio *adj* evidentiary
proceder *v* proceed
procedimiento *nm* procedure, proceeding
procedimiento expeditivo *nm* summary proceeding
procedimiento judicial *nm* judicial proceeding, trial
     procedure
procedimiento oral *nm* oral proceedings
procedimiento sumario *nm* summary proceeding
proceso *nm* trial
proceso debido *nm* due process
propiedad *nf* property
propio *adj* proper, one's own, proprietary
propósito *nm* intention, purpose
prórroga de suspensión *nf* extension of period of stay
proveer *v* provide for, supply
prueba *nf* proof, evidence
prueba admisible *nf* admissible evidence
prueba circunstancial *nf* circumstantial evidence
prueba de oída *nf* hearsay
prueba documental *nf* documentary evidence
prueba física *nf* physical evidence
prueba real *nf* exhibit, physical evidence
puñal *nm* knife, dagger
puñalada *nf* stab wound
punción *nf* puncture, stab wound
pupilo *nm* conservatee

queja *nf* complaint, grievance
querella *nf* lawsuit, suit, complaint
ratificación de una decisión *nf* affirmance of
    a decision
reanudar *v* resume
rebatible *adj* rebuttable
rebatir *v* rebut
rebeldía *nf* contempt of court
rechazar *v* deny, reject, overrule
rechazar una objeción *v* overrule an objection
rechazo *nm* denial, rejection
reclamación *nf* claim
reclamante *nm* claimant
reclamar *v* claim, demand
reclamo *nm* claim, demand
reconocimiento de pago del fallo *nm* acknowledgment
    of satisfaction of judgment
recurrente *nm* appellant
recurrir *v* appeal
recurso *nm* appeal, recourse
recurso de clase *nm* class action
recusación *nf* recusal, disqualification
recusación del jurado *nf* jury challenge
recusar *v* recuse
reenviar un caso a un tribunal *v* remand
refutable *adj* rebuttable
refutación *nf* rebuttal
registrarar *v* search
registro *nm* search
registro corporal *nm* bodily search, body search
reglamento interno *nm* bylaws

rehabilitación *nf* rehabilitation
rehabilitar *v* rehabilitate
rendirse *v* surrender, turn oneself in
renunciación *nf* waiver
renunciar a un derecho *v* waive a right
repregunta *nf* cross-examination
repreguntar *v* cross-examine
representante *nm* representative
representante legal *nm* legal representative
representar *v* represent
rescindir *v* rescind
rescisión *nf* rescission
resolver *v* resolve, rescind, terminate
responsabilidad *nf* responsibility, liability
responsabilidad legal *nf* legal liability
responsable *adj* responsible, liable
respuesta escrita *nf* written answer
resumen *nm* abstract *(summary)*
resumen de fallo *nm* abstract of judgment
retención de ingresos *nf* garnishment, income
      withholding
retención directa de ingresos *nf* direct income
      withholding
retirar *v* withdraw, revoke
retrasar *v* delay
retraso *nm* delay
reunir pruebas *v* collect evidence
revelar *v* disclose
revisar *v* revise, review, search
revisión judicial *nf* judicial review
revocación *nf* revocation, withdrawal, repeal

revocar *v* revoke, withdraw, repeal, reverse *(a judgment)*
sala de audiencia *nf* courtroom
salir juntos *v* date, go out together
salvo acuerdo en contrario *adv* unless otherwise agreed
sanción *nf* penalty, sanction
secretariado del tribunal *nm* court clerk's office
secretario del tribunal *nm* court clerk
segunda repregunta *nf* re-cross examination
sentencia *nf* judgment
separación de acciones procesales *nf* severance of proceedings
SIDA *nm* AIDS (Acquired Immune Deficiency Syndrome)
sin perjuicio *adj/adv* without prejudice
sistema contencioso *nm* adversarial system
sobornar *v* suborn, bribe
soborno *nm* subornation, bribery
sobreseimiento *nm* dismissal
sobreseir *v* dismiss
solicitar *v* apply, petition, request
solicitud *nf* application, petition, request
sorprender *v* surprise
sorpresa *nf* surprise
sostener *v* argue, maintain
suma *nf* sum, amount
sumario *nm* summation, brief
suponer *v* suppose, presume, assume
suspender *v* adjourn
suspendido *adj* adjourned
suspensión *nm* adjournment
tangible *adj* tangible

taquígrafo judicial *nm* court reporter
tener la intención de *v* intend
término de prescripción *nm* statute of limitations
testamento *nm* will
testigo *nm* witness
testigo adverso *nm* adverse witness
testimonio *nm* testimony
trámite *nm* procedure
transacción *nf* settlement, compromise
transcripción *nf* transcript
transferencia de la causa a un tribunal federal *nf*
    removal of case to federal court
transferir *v* transfer, assign
trastorno mental *nm* mental disorder
tratado *nm* treaty
traumático *adj* traumatic
tribunal *nm* court
tribunal de apelaciones *nm* court of appeals
tribunal de distrito *nm* district court
tribunal de primera instancia *nm* trial court
tribunal de segunda instancia *nm* court of appeals
tribunal sucesorio *nm* surrogate court
usuario *nm* user
válido *adj* valid
valor *nm* value
valor probatorio *nm* probative value
valorar *v* value, appraise
vencer *v* expire
vencido *adj* expired
vencimiento *nm* expiration
veredicto *nm* verdict

vicio *nm* vice, addiction
vigente *adj* in force, in effect
vinculante *adj* binding
visa *nf* visa
vista *nf* hearing
vocero *nm* spokesman
vocero del jurado *nm* foreman of jury
voluntariamente *adv* voluntarily, willingly
voluntario *adj* voluntary

DERECHO COMERCIAL
COMMERCIAL LAW

El **derecho comercial** abarca las relaciones **contractuales** y de **negocios**, las **finanzas**, la **banca**, las **inversiones**, los **seguros**, y las normas que rigen la venta de **bienes** y **servicios** a los **consumidores**.

abastecer *v* supply
abastecimiento *nm* supply
abonar *v* pay
acaparar *v* corner the market
acción *nf* share
acciones *nf* stock
acciones ordinarias *nf* common stock
aceptación *nf* acceptance
acreedor *nm* creditor
acreedor privilegiado *nm* secured creditor
activo *nm* asset
activo exigible *nm* receivable
activo líquido *nm* liquid asset
activos fijos *nm* fixed assets, capital assets
activos permanentes *nm* fixed assets
acuerdo *nm* agreement, contract
adelantado *adj* early, in advance
adelanto en efectivo *nm* cash advance
adquirir *v* acquire, obtain, purchase
adquisición *nf* acquisition, purchase

agencia *nf* agency

agencia de calificación de crédito *nf* credit rating
    agency, credit reporting agency

agencia de cobranza *nf* collection agency

agencia de reporte y clasificación de crédito *nf*
    credit bureau

agente *nm* agent

agente autorizado *nm* authorized agent, franchisee

agilizar *v* streamline

ahorrar *v* save

ahorros *nm* savings

alquiler *nm* rent

amortización *nf* amortization

anticipo en efectivo *nm* cash advance

anulación de contrato *nf* rescission of contract,
    termination of contract

anulación de deuda *nf* cancellation of debt

año calendario *nm* calendar year

año civil *nm* calendar year

año fiscal *nm* fiscal year

apoderado *nm* nominee, attorney-in-fact

apreciación *nm* appreciation

arancel *nm* tariff, customs, duty

arbitraje *nm* arbitration

arrendamiento *nm* lease

arrendar *v* lease

artículos de lujo *nm* luxury goods

asegurado *adj* insured

asunto *nm* matter, affair

auditoría *nf* audit

aviso por escrito *nm* written notice

banca *nf* banking
banca electrónica *nf* online banking, e-banking
banco *nm* bank
banco central *nm* central bank
banco comercial *nm* commercial bank
banco de inversión *nm* merchant bank, investment bank
basándose en lo devengado *adv* on an accrual basis
beca *nf* scholarship
beneficiar *v* benefit
beneficiario *nm* beneficiary, payee
beneficio *nm* benefit
beneficios de desempleo *nm* unemployment benefits
bien *nm* property, asset
bienes *nm* goods, property, assets
bienes de consumo *nm* consumer goods
bienes de marca pirateados *nm* pirated copyright goods
bienes depreciables *nm* depreciable property
bienes exentos *nm* exempt goods, exempt assets
bolsa de productos básicos *nf* commodity exchange
bolsa de valores *nf* stock exchange
bono *nm* bond
bono de ahorro *nm* savings bond
bono municipal *nm* municipal bond
buena fe *nf* good faith
bursátil *adj* pertaining to stock exchange
bursatilización *nf* securitization
buzón *nm* mailbox
cajero automático *nm* automated teller machine
    (ATM), cash machine
calificación de crédito *nf* credit score, credit rating
cancelar una deuda *v* cancel a debt, retire a debt

Commercial Law

capital *nm* capital, principal
capitalizar *v* capitalize
carga *nf* consignment, shipment
cargamento *nm* shipment
cargas sociales *nf* payroll taxes
cargo por sobrelímite *nm* overlimit charge
carta de crédito *nf* letter of credit
carta poder *nf* proxy statement
categoría de crédito *nf* credit profile
certificado *nm* certificate
certificado de depósito (CD) *nm* certificate of
   deposit (CD)
certificado de depósitos en custodia *nm* depositary
   receipt
cesión *nf* assignment
cheque *nm* check
cheque al portador *nm* bearer check
cheque cancelado *nm* cancelled check
cheque certificado *nm* certified check
cheque de cajero *nm* bank check, cashier's check
cheque de sueldo *nm* paycheck
cheque de viajero *nm* traveler's check
cheque personal *nm* personal check
ciclo de facturación *nm* billing cycle
cláusula *nf* clause
cláusula de abstención de competencia *nf* no-
   competition clause
cláusula resolutiva *nf* cancellation clause
clave personal *nf* password
cliente *nm* client, customer
cobrar *v* charge *(a price, fee, etc.)*, cash *(a check)*

cobro *nm* charge
cobro por demora *nm* late charge
cobro por tardanza *nm* late charge
Código Tributario *nm* Tax Code, Internal Revenue
    Code
cofirmante *nm* cosigner
colateral *nm* collateral
comerciable *adj* merchantable
comercio *nm* commerce
comercio electrónico *nm* e-commerce
comisión *nf* commission
comité de inversiones *nm* investment committee
compañía *nf* company
compañía de informes de consumidores *nf* consumer
    reporting company
compañía privada *nf* private company
compañía punto.com *nf* dot-com company
compensación *nf* compensation
compensación monetaria *nm* monetary compensation
competencia *nf* competition
competencia desleal *nf* unfair competition
compra *nf* purchase
comprador *nm* buyer
comprar *v* purchase
compraventa *nf* agreement for sale and purchase
concesión *nf* concession
concesión comercial *nf* franchise
concurrencia *nf* competition
concurrente *nm* competitor
congelar *(activos, depósitos, etc.)* *v* freeze *(assets,*
    deposits, etc.)

Commercial Law

consejero de crédito *nm* credit counselor
consejero de inversiones *nm* investment counselor
consejero financiero *nm* financial advisor
consignación *nf* shipment, consignment
consignatario *nm* consignee
constancia de liberación de hipoteca *nf* release note
constituir legalmente *(una sociedad)* *v* incorporate
   (a company)
consultor financiero colegiado *nm* chartered financial
   consultant
consumidor *nm* consumer
contabilidad *nf* accounting
contable *nm* accountant
contador *nm* bookkeeper, accountant
contador público *nm* certified public accountant (CPA)
contante *nm* cash
contrademanda *nf* counterclaim
contraoferta *nf* counteroffer
contraprestación *nm* consideration
contraseña *nf* password
contratante *nm* contracting party, contractor
contratista *nm* contractor
contratista independiente *nm* independent contractor
contrato *nm* contract
contrato de garantía *nm* contract of guarantee
contrato de indemnidad *nm* contract of indemnity
contrato de negocios *nm* business contract
contrato de palabra *nm* verbal contract
contrato de servicio *nm* service contract
contrato de tarjeta de crédito *nm* credit card
   agreement

contrato de venta *nm* contract of sale
contrato oral, verbal *nm* oral contract
contrato por escrito *nm* written contract
contribuyente *nm* taxpayer
convenio *nm* agreement, contract, convention
convertible *adj* convertible
cooperativa de crédito *nf* credit union
corporación *nf* corporation
corredor *nm* broker
correo *nm* mail
correo electrónico *nm* e-mail
cosignatario *nm* cosigner
costar *v* cost
costear *v* defray, pay for
costo *nm* cost
costo financiero *nm* finance charge
costos de negociación *nm* transaction fees,
    transaction costs
crédito *nm* credit
crédito al consumidor *nm* consumer credit
crédito tributario *nm* tax credit
cuenta *nf* account, bill, invoice
cuenta bancaria *nf* bank account
cuenta conjunta *nf* joint account
cuenta corriente *nf* current account
cuenta de ahorros *nf* savings account
cuenta de cheques *nf* checking account
cuenta de crédito renovable *nf* revolving account
cuenta de gastos *nf* expense account
cuenta de gastos flexible *nf* flexible spending
    account (FSA)

cuenta de inversiones *nf* investment account

cuenta de pérdidas y ganancias *nf* profit and loss account

cuenta de retiro individual *nf* individual retirement account (IRA)

cuenta del mercado monetario *nf* money market account

cuenta incobrable anulada *nf* write-off account

cuentas pagaderas *nf* accounts payable

cumplimiento *nm* compliance

cuota *nm* fee

cuota annual *nf* annual fee

cupo *nm* quota

de buena fe *adj/adv* bona fide

deber *v* owe

débito *nm* debit

declaración de impuestos *nf* tax return

declaración de impuestos conjunta *nf* joint return

declaración de impuestos enmendada/corregida *nf* amended return

declaración electrónica *(de impuestos)* *nf* e-filing *(of income tax)*

deducción *nf* deduction

deducción por donación caritativa *nf* charitable contribution deduction

deducciones detalladas *nf* itemized deductions

deducciones detalladas ajustadas *nf* adjusted itemized deductions

defensor del contribuyente *nm* taxpayer advocate

defraudar *v* defraud, swindle

demora *nf* delay, lateness

demorado *adj* delayed
dependiente *adj/nm* dependent
depósito *nm* deposit
depósito a plazo *nm* time deposit
depósito nocturno *nm* night deposit
depreciación *nf* depreciation
depreciación acelerada *nf* accelerated depreciation
derecho *nm* right, law, fee or payment due
derecho comercial *nm* commercial law
derecho de contratos *nm* contract law
derecho de retención *nm* lien
derecho de sociedades *nm* company law
derecho impositivo *nm* tax law
derecho tributario *nm* tax law
derechos de autor *nm* royalties
derechos del consumidor *nm* consumer rights
derivados *nm* derivatives
descubierto *nm* overdraft
descuento *nm* discount
desgravable *adj* tax deductible
despido temporal *nm* layoff
destinatario *nm* recipient, consignee, addressee
deuda *nf* debt
deuda de consumidor *nf* consumer debt
deuda incobrable *nf* bad debt
deuda tributaria *nf* tax liability
deudor *nm* debtor
devengar *v* accrue, accumulate
días hábiles *nm* business days
días laborales *nm* business days, work days
dictamen con salvedades *nm* qualified audit opinion

dictamen de auditoría *nm* audit opinion
diferendo comercial *nm* commercial dispute
distribuidor *nm* distributor
distribuidor automático *nm* vending machine
diversificar *v* diversify
dividendo *nm* dividend
dividendo ordinario *nm* ordinary dividend
dividendos brutos *nm* gross dividends
divulgación *nf* disclosure
doble contabilidad *nf* double counting
doble facturación *nf* double billing
doble utilización *nf* double dipping
dueño de casa *nm* homeowner
efectivo *nm* cash
efecto a cobrar *nm* receivable
embarcar *v* ship, embark
emitir (*préstamos, bonos, etc.*) *v* issue, float *(loans, bonds, etc.)*
empleado casero *nm* homeworker
empresa *nf* enterprise, company
empresa matriz *nm* parent company
en bruto *adj* gross
en especie *adj/adv* in kind
en línea *adj* online
en mora *adj* delinquent
en quiebra *adj* bankrupt
encabezamiento de documento *nm* heading of document
endosar *v* endorse
endoso *nm* endorsement
enganche *nm* down payment

engañoso *adj* deceptive
entablar queja *v* grieve, file a complaint
entrante *adj* incoming
envío *nm* consignment, shipment, remittance
error de facturación *nm* billing error
escritura de sociedad *nm* articles of association
estado contable consolidado *nm* consolidated
    financial statement
estado de cuenta *nm* bank statement
estado financiero *nm* financial statement
estados financieros históricos *nm* historic financial
    statements
estrategia de inversión *nf* investment strategy
evasión *nf* evasion
exención de impuestos *nf* tax exemption
exenciones personales *nf* personal exemptions
exento de impuestos *adj* tax exempt
exoneración de impuestos *nf* tax exemption
extinción de contrato *nf* discharge of contract
extinción de deuda *nf* discharge of debt
fabricante *nm* manufacturer
facsímile *nm* facsimile
factura *nf* invoice
facturación excesiva *nf* overbilling
facturar *v* bill, invoice
fallido *adj* bankrupt
fax *nm* fax
fecha de vencimiento *nf* due date, date of expiry,
    maturity date
fecha límite *nf* deadline, due date
fecha tope *nf* deadline, due date

fiduciario *nm* fiduciary
filial *nf* affiliate
financiación *nf* funding, financing
financiar *v* finance
finanza *nf* finance
flete *nm* freight
flujo de liquidez *nm* cash flow
fondo *nm* fund
fondo de cobertura *nm* hedge fund
fondo de inversión *nm* investment fund, mutual fund
fondo fiduciario *nm* trust fund
fondo mutuo *nm* mutual fund
fondo para jubilados y pensionados *nm* pension fund
fondos *nm* funds
formulario *nm* form
franquicia *nf* franchise, exemption
franquicia aduanera *nf* exemption from customs duties
franquicia de impuestos *nf* tax exemption
franquiciado *nm* franchisee
franquiciador *nm* franchisor
fusión *(de sociedades)* *nf* merger *(of companies)*
fusiones y adquisiciones *nf* mergers and acquisitions
ganancia *nf* profit
ganancia neta *nf* net profit
ganancia o pérdida de capital *nf* capital gain or loss
ganancias ilegales *nf* unlawful gains
ganga *nf* bargain
garantía *nf* warranty, guarantee
gasto deducible de impuestos *nm* tax deduction
gastos de capital *nm* capital expenditure
gastos de intereses *nm* interest expenses

gastos de mudanza *nm* moving expenses
gastos empresarios *nm* business expenses
gerente *nm* manager
gestión *nm* management
girado *nm* drawee
girador *nm* drawer
giro *nm* money order, draft
gravamen *nm* lien
guardería *nf* day-care center
haber *nm* asset, worth
haber patrimonial *nm* net worth
hipoteca *nf* mortgage
hipoteca de primer rango *nf* first mortgage
hipoteca revertida *nf* reverse mortgage
historial de crédito *nm* credit history
hoja de balance *nf* balance sheet
hombre de negocios *nm* businessman
honorario *nm* fee
horas laborales *nf* business hours
impuesto *nm* tax
impuesto al uso *nm* use tax
impuesto de consumo *nm* excise tax
impuesto de seguro social *nm* Social Security tax
impuesto de valor añadido (IVA) *nm* value added
     tax (VAT)
impuesto debido a la nómina de empleados *nm*
     employment tax, payroll tax
impuesto escolar *nm* school tax
impuesto estatal *nm* state tax
impuesto estimado *nm* estimated tax
impuesto Medicare *nm* Medicare tax

impuesto mínimo alternativo *nm* alternative
    minimum tax
impuesto progresivo *nm* progressive tax
impuesto retenido *nm* withholding tax
impuesto sobre bienes inmuebles *nm* property tax
impuesto sobre donaciones *nm* gift tax
impuesto sobre el volumen de negocios *nm*
    turnover tax
impuesto sobre la renta *nm* income tax
impuesto sobre las ganancias de capital *nm* capital
    gains tax
impuesto sobre las ventas *nm* sales tax
impuesto sucesorio *nm* estate tax, death tax
impuestos locales *nm* local taxes
incumplimiento *nm* default, breach, non-compliance
incumplimiento de contrato *nm* breach of contract
incumplimiento de garantía *nm* breach of warranty
incurrir *v* incur
indemnización *nf* indemnification, compensation
indemnizar *v* indemnify, compensate
informe anual *nm* annual report
informe de crédito *nm* credit report
informe de sociedad *nm* company report
informe semestral *nm* half-year report
ingreso *nm* income
ingreso bruto *nm* gross income
ingreso bruto ajustado *nm* adjusted gross income
ingreso de intereses *nm* interest income
ingreso de seguro social *nm* Social Security income
ingreso salarial *nm* earned income

ingresos devengados en el extranjero *nm* foreign
    earned income
ingresos netos *nm* net earnings
inscripción *nf* registration, enrollment
insolvencia *nf* insolvency
insolvente *adj* insolvent
instantáneo *adj* instant, real-time
instrumento *nm* instrument
instrumento de inversión *nm* investment vehicle
interés *nm* interest
interés capitalizado *nm* capitalized interest
interés compuesto *nm* compound interest
intereses devengados *nm* accrued interest
inventario *nm* inventory
inversión *nf* investment
inversión de alto riesgo *nf* high-risk investment
inversionista *nm* investor
inversor *nm* investor
invertir *v* invest
investigador fiscal *nm* financial investigator *(IRS agent)*
jefe de familia *nm* head of household
lavado de dinero *nm* money laundering
letra de cambio *nf* bill of exchange, draft
letra del tesoro *nf* treasury bill
liberación *nf* discharge
libranza *nf* money order
libro mayor *nm* ledger
licencia *nf* license
licencia comercial *nf* business license
límite de crédito *nm* credit limit
línea de crédito *nf* credit line

Commercial Law

liquidación *nf* liquidation
liquidar *v* liquidate
liquidez *nf* liquidity
litigio comercial *nm* commercial dispute, commercial litigation
lucro *nm* profit
mandado *nm* agent, errand
mandatario *nm* agent
mandato *nm* agency
materia prima *nf* raw material
matrícula *nf* registration
matrícula de comercio *nf* business license
mayoreo *nm* wholesale
membrete *nm* letterhead
mensajero *nm* courier, messenger
mensajes de voz *nm* voicemail
menudeo *nm* retail
mercado *nm* market
mercado de valores *nm* stock market
mercado monetario *nm* money market
mercado negro *nm* black market
mercadotécnica *nf* marketing
mercancía *nf* merchandise
moneda corriente *nf* legal tender
monopolizar *v* monopolize
moras *nf* arrears
morosidad *nf* delinquency *(in payments)*
móvil *adj* mobile, wireless
mujer de negocios *nf* businesswoman
multa por declaración retrasada *nf* late filing penalty
negociante *nm* merchant, dealer, trader

negocio *nm* business

negocio en casa *nm* home-based business

neto *adj* net

neto de impuestos *adv* after tax

nota promisoria *nf* promissory note

nulo *adj* null, void

numerario *nm* cash

número de identificación personal *nm* personal
identification number (PIN)

Número de Seguro Social *nm* Social Security
Number (SSN)

obligación *nf* debenture, obligation

oferente *nm* offeror

oferta *nf* offer, offering, supply

oferta pública inicial *nf* initial public offering (IPO)

offshore *adj* offshore

oficina a domicilio *nm* home office

ofrecer *v* offer

opción de compra *(de un valor a precio fijo en
determinada fecha futura)* *nf* call option *(option
enabling holder to buy a security at a fixed price
by a set date in future)*

operación *nf* operation, transaction

operación financiera *nf* financial transaction

operación garantizada *nf* secured transaction

pagadero *adj* payable

pagadero a la vista *adj* payable at sight

pagador *nm* payor

pagaré *nm* promissory note, IOU

pago *nm* payment

pago en exceso *nm* overpayment

pago global *nm* lump-sum payment, balloon payment

pago insuficiente *nm* underpayment

pago mínimo *nm* minimum payment

pago retrasado *nm* late payment

parte contratante *nf* contracting party

patrimonio *nm* worth, assets, inheritance, estate

pedir prestado *v* borrow

penalidad *nf* penalty

penalidad por pago insuficiente *nf* underpayment penalty

penalidad por retiro anticipado *nf* early withdrawal penalty

pensión *nf* pension

pequeño negocio *nm* small business

pérdida *nf* loss

pérdida o ganancia no realizada *nf* unrealized loss or profit

Plan 401(k) *nm* 401(k) Plan

plan de adquisición de acciones para empleados *nm* employee stock plan

plan de jubilación *nm* retirement plan

plazo de reembolso *nm* repayment period

política de confidencialidad *nf* privacy policy

por cobrar *adj* collect

portador *nm* bearer

precio *nm* price

precio de adquisición *nm* purchase price

precio de compra *nm* purchase price

precio de ejercicio *(de un contrato de opciones)* *nm* exercise price *(price set in an option contract)*

precio de liquidación *nm* distressed price

precio de venta *nm* sale price
precombinado *adj* prepackaged
preferente *adj* preferred
premio *nm* prize, bonus
preparador de formularios de impuestos *nm* tax
    preparer
presentar *v* present
prestación *nf* benefit, service
prestación marginal *nf* fringe benefit
prestamista *nm* moneylender
préstamo *nm* loan
préstamo puente *nm* bridge loan, swing loan
prestar *v* lend
prestatario *nm* borrower
presupuesto *nm* budget
presupuesto equilibrado *nm* balanced budget
prima *nf* bonus
prima de seguro *nf* insurance premium
privación *nm* hardship
pro forma *adj* pro forma
producción *nf* production
producir *v* produce
productividad *nf* productivity
producto *nm* product, proceeds
producto básico *nm* commodity
propina *nf* tip, gratuity
propuesta *nf* bid, proposal
prorrata *adj* pro rata
prorratear *v* prorate
prospecto *nm* prospectus
proveedor *nm* supplier

proveer *v* supply
publicidad *nf* publicity
publicidad fraudulenta *nm* false advertising
quiebra *nf* bankruptcy
reabastecer *v* replenish, resupply
realizar *v* realize
recargo *nm* late fee, surcharge
recaudador de impuestos *nm* tax collector
recibo *nm* receipt
rédito *nm* return, yield
rédito de inversión *nm* return on investment
reducción fiscal *nf* tax relief
reembolsar *v* reimburse
reembolso *nm* refund, reimbursement
reembolso de impuestos *nm* tax refund
refugio fiscal *nm* tax shelter
reintegrar *v* repay
remitente *nm* sender
renovación de contrato *nf* renewal of contract
renta *nf* rent, income
rentar *v* rent
renuncia *nf* resignation
renunciar *v* resign
reorganización *nf* restructuring, reorganization
reparto de ganancias *nm* profit sharing
rescindir *v* rescind
rescisión de contrato *nf* rescission of contract,
    termination of contract
resguardo *nm* collateral
responsabilidad legal *nf* legal liability
responsabilidad limitada *nf* limited liability

responsabilidad por productos defectuosos *nf*
    product liability
responsable de préstamos *nm* loan officer
retención adicional de impuesto *nf* backup
    withholding
retener *v* withhold
retirar *(fondos)* *v* withdraw, draw *(funds)*
retiro *nm* withdrawal, retirement
retiro anticipado *nm* premature withdrawal
retiro indebido *nm* unauthorized withdrawal
retribución *nf* compensation
saldar *v* pay off
saldo *nm* balance
saldo anterior *nm* previous balance
saldo deudor *nm* debit balance
saldo diario *nm* daily balance
saldo diario promedio *nm* average daily balance
saldo pendiente *nm* outstanding balance
secreto comercial *nm* trade secret
seguridad social *nf* Social Security
seguro *nm* insurance
seguro de responsabilidad legal *nm* liability
    insurance
seguro de vida *nm* life insurance
seguro de vida a plazo *nm* term life insurance
seguro sobre el crédito *nm* credit insurance
servicio al cliente *nm* customer service
servicios bancarios en línea *nm* online banking
sin fines de lucro *adj* nonprofit
sobrecargo *nm* surcharge
sobregirar *v* overdraw

Commercial Law

sobregiro *nm* overdraft
sociedad *nf* company
sociedad anónima *nf* corporation
sociedad controlante *nm* parent company
sociedad cotizante *nf* publicly traded company
sociedad de inversiones *nf* investment company
sociedad distribuidora *nf* distributorship
sociedad matriz *nm* parent company
socio *nm* partner, associate
solvente *adj* solvent
subasta *nf* auction
subsidiaria *nf* subsidiary
sujeto a impuesto *adj* taxable
sujeto a impuesto diferido *adj* tax deferred
suspender un pago *v* stop payment
tarifa *nf* schedule
tarjeta de crédito *nf* credit card
tarjeta de débito *nf* debit card
tasa *nf* rate
tasa de cambio *nm* exchange rate
tasa de descuento *nf* discount rate
tasa de interés *nf* interest rate
tasa de mercado *nf* market rate
tasa de rédito *nf* rate of return
tasa fija *nf* flat rate
tasa impositiva *nf* tax rate
tasa LIBOR *nf* London Interbank Offered Rate (LIBOR)
tasa periódica diaria *nf* daily periodic rate
tasa porcentual anual *nf* annual percentage rate (APR)
tasación *nf* assessment
tasación impositiva *nf* tax assessment

tasador *nm* assessor, receiver
temprano *adj/adv* early
titular beneficiario *nm* beneficial owner
titulización *nf* securitization
toma hostil *nf* hostile takeover
tramo fiscal *nm* tax bracket
transferencia *nf* transfer, assignment
transferencia de fondos *nf* money transfer
transferencia electrónica de fondos *nf* electronic
    funds transfer (EFT)
traspasar *(un saldo anterior)* *v* carry over *(a balance)*
tratado fiscal *nm* tax treaty
tribunal de impuestos *nm* tax court
tribunal de insolvencia *nm* bankruptcy court
tribunal de quiebra *nm* bankruptcy court
trimestre civil *nm* calendar quarter
utilidad *nf* profit
utilidad neta *nf* net profit
valor *nm* value
valor contable *nm* book value
valor de mercado *nm* market value
valor justo de mercado *nm* fair market value (FMV)
valor nominal *nm* par value
valor pasado a perdidas *nm* write-off
valorar *v* assess, appraise
valores *nm* securities
vencimiento *nm* maturity
vendedor *nm* seller, vendor
vender *v* sell
venta *nf* sale
ventas brutas *nf* gross sales

ventas netas *nf* net sales
vigente *adj* in effect, in force
vivienda *nf* dwelling, housing
volumen operado *nm* trading volume
warrant *(certificado que da derecho a comprar valores a precio fijo en el futuro)* *nm* warrant *(certificate issued to holders of securities giving them the right to buy securities at a set price in future)*

Derecho Comercial

DERECHO PENAL
CRIMINAL LAW

El **derecho penal** tiene que ver con aquellos actos que la sociedad considera **castigables**. Según el antiguo principio *nulla poena sine lege* ("no hay crimen sin ley") solo se pueden castigar aquellos actos que han sido definidos por la ley como penables. Existen disposiciones contra el **doble enjuiciamiento** por la misma causa para evitar que una persona **exculpada** sea juzgada otra vez por el mismo delito. El **acusado** que se encuentra **enjuiciado** generalmente goza de ciertas garantías procesales para su **defensa** según los códigos de **procedimiento penal**. Si resulta **condenado** (declarado culpable) recibirá un castigo según la gravedad del delito cometido. Las penas varían desde una **multa** por haber cometido un delito menor hasta el **encarcelamiento**, o inclusive la pena de muerte, por delitos mayores. En los Estados Unidos, esta materia se rige por leyes estatales y federales.

a sabiendas *adv* knowingly
abogado defensor *nm* defense attorney
absolución *nf* acquittal
absolver *v* acquit
absuelto *adj* acquitted
abuso sexual *nm* sexual abuse
aceptación de responsabilidad *nf* acceptance of
    responsibility

acoso *nm* harassment

acoso sexual *nm* sexual harassment

acuerdo de cooperación *nm* cooperation agreement

acumulación de delitos *nf* joinder of offenses

acusado *adj/nm* accused; *nm* defendant

acusación *nf* accusation, charge

acusación formal *nm* indictment

admisión *nf* admission

advertencia según el caso Miranda *nf* Miranda
warning *(Ver Anexo 2 / see Appendix 2)*

afirmación *nf* statement, affirmation

agente de vigilancia de libertad condicional *nm*
probation officer

agente policíaco encubierto *nm* undercover police
officer

agravado *adj* aggravated

agraviado *nm* injured party

agresión *nf* assault

agresión con arma mortífera *nf* assault with a deadly
weapon

agresor sexual *nm* sexual predator

ajuste de cuentas *nm* settling of accounts

alcahuete *nm* pimp

alcaldía *nf* misdemeanor court

alcoholemia *nf* Blood Alcohol Level (BAC)

alguacil *nm* sheriff, bailiff

allanamiento de morada *nm* burglary

allanar *v* search *(premises)*

allanamiento *nm* breaking and entering, search of
premises

alteración del orden público *nm* disturbing the peace

alterar *v* alter, tamper with
amnistía *nf* amnesty
ánimo *nm* intent, intention
antecedentes penales *nm* criminal record, criminal
    history
apuñalar *v* stab
arma *nf* weapon
arma de fuego *nf* firearm
arma mortífera *nf* deadly weapon
arrestar *v* arrest
asaltante *nm* assailant, mugger
asesinato *nm* murder
asesinato agravado o premeditado *nm* first-degree
    murder
asesino *nm* murderer
audiencia de deportación *nf* deportation hearing
ausentismo escolar *nm* truancy
auto-defensa *nf* self-defense
autoinculpación *nf* self-incrimination
autor *(de delito) nm* perpetrator *(of an offense)*
autor intelectual *nm* mastermind
averiguar *v* investigate, find out
bala *nf* bullet
balazo *nm* gunshot
bigamia *nf* bigamy
bígamo *nm* bigamist
blanqueo de dinero *nm* money laundering
boleta por infracción de tránsito *nf* traffic ticket
cachear *v* frisk
cadena perpetua *nf* life sentence
cárcel *nf* jail

Criminal Law

carga de la prueba *nf* burden of proof
cargo *nm* charge
carterista *nm* pickpocket
castigo *nm* punishment
causa inmediata *nf* proximate cause
causa superveniente *nf* supervening cause
celador *nm* prison guard
celda *nf* cell
celda de detención temporal *nf* holding cell
centro correccional *nm* correctional center
ciberdelito *nm* cybercrime
circunstancias agravantes *nf* aggravating circumstances
circunstancias eximientes *nf* extenuating circumstances
citar *v* summon, subpoena
clemencia *nf* clemency
coacción *nf* duress, coercion
coacción física *nf* physical restraint
coartada *nf* alibi
cobranza civil *nf* civil collections
co-conspirador *nm* co-conspirator
código de procedimientos penales *nm* code of criminal
       procedure
coerción *nf* duress, coercion
cohecho *nm* coercion
cometer *(un delito)* *v* commit *(a crime)*
comparendo *nm* subpoena
cómplice *nm* accomplice
Concentración de Alcohol en la Sangre (CAS) *nf*
       Blood Alcohol Level (BAC)
condena *nf* conviction
condena anterior *nf* prior conviction

condenado *adj* convicted
condenar *v* convict
conducir en estado de ebriedad *v* driving while
intoxicated (DWI)
conducta pertinente *nf* relevant conduct
confesión *nf* confession
confiscar *v* seize, confiscate
conjurador *nm* conspirator
conjurar *v* conspire
conspiración *nf* conspiracy
conspirador *nm* conspirator
conspirador con participación menor *nm* minor
participant
conspirador con participación mínima *nm* minimal
participant
conspirar *v* conspire
contrabandear *v* smuggle
contrabandista *nm* smuggler
contrabando *nm* contraband, smuggling
convenio declaratorio *nm* plea agreement, plea bargain
convicto *adj* convicted
cooperación con la fiscalía *nf* cooperation with the
prosecution
corrupción *nf* corruption
crimen de odio *nm* hate crime
crimen organizado *nm* organized crime
crimen pasional *nm* crime of passion
cuerda de sospechosos *nf* lineup
culpable *adj* guilty
cumplir sentencia *v* serve a sentence
custodia judicial *nf* custody *(of a person)*

Criminal Law

daño corporal *nm* physical harm

declaración *nf* statement

declaración condicional de culpabilidad *nf* conditional plea of guilty

declaración jurada escrita *nf* affidavit

declaraciones engañosas *nf* false statements, false pretenses

declaraciones fraudulentas *nf* false statements, false pretenses

decomiso *nm* forfeiture

defensa *nf* defense

defensa afirmativa *nf* affirmative defense

defensa propia *nf* self-defense

defensor de oficio *nm* public defender

defensor público *nm* public defender

delator *nm* informer

deliberadamente *adv* intentionally, deliberately

delincuente *nm* offender

delincuente juvenil *nm* juvenile offender

delito *nm* offense

delito capital *nm* capital offense

delito de incendio *nm* arson

delito de vileza moral *nm* crime of moral turpitude

delito federal *nm* federal offense

delito grave *nm* felony

delito grave con circunstancias agravantes *nm* aggravated felony

delito juvenil anterior *nm* prior juvenile offense

delito mayor *nm* felony

delito menor *nm* misdemeanor

delito violento *nm* crime of violence

denuncia *nf* complaint *(criminal)*
deportable *adj* deportable
deportación *nf* deportation
deportar *v* deport
depredador sexual *nm* sexual predator
desfalco *nm* embezzlement
desmantelamiento de vehículo *nm* auto stripping
detective *nm* detective
detención *nf* detention
detención domiciliaria *nf* home detention
detención ilegal o injustificada *nf* false imprisonment
detención preventiva *nf* pretrial detention
documento inculpatorio *nm* indictment
duda razonable *nf* reasonable doubt
dúplica *nf* rebuttal
ebriedad *nf* intoxication, drunkenness
emplazamiento *nm* summons, subpoena
emplazar a comparecer *v* summon, subpoena
en rebeldía *adv* in absentia
encarcelamiento *nm* imprisonment, confinement
encarcelar *v* confine, imprison
encausar *v* try, prosecute
encubridor *nm* accessory after the fact
engaño *nm* deceit, fraud
enjuiciar *v* prosecute, try
entrada ilícita *nf* criminal trespass
entrega *nf* surrender
entrega voluntaria *nf* voluntary surrender
escalador nocturno *nm* burglar
esposas *nf* handcuffs
estado *nm* state, status

Criminal Law

estafa *nf* fraud, swindle

estafar *v* defraud, swindle

estupro *(relaciones sexuales con un menor)* *nm* statutory rape *(sexual relations with a minor)*

exacción *nf* extortion, blackmail

examen del testigo por el fiscal *nm* questioning of witness on direct examination

exclusión de pruebas *nf* suppression of evidence

exculpado *adj* acquitted

exculpar *v* acquit

exhibición obscena *nf* indecent exposure

exhibicionismo *nf* indecent exposure

exonerar *v* exonerate, acquit

expediente de apelación *nm* record on appeal

expulsable *adj* deportable, removable

expulsar *(a un extranjero del país)* *v* remove, deport *(an alien from the country)*

expurgar *v* expunge

extorción *nf* extortion, blackmail

fallo absolutorio *nm* acquittal

falsario *nm* counterfeiter

falsificación *nf* forgery

falsificación de moneda *nf* counterfeiting

falsificado *adj* counterfeit, forged

falsificador *nm* forger

falta *nf* fault, infraction

fiador *nm* bailor

fiador judicial *nm* bail bondsman

fianza compuesta *nf* bail package

fianza de descarcelación *nf* bail

fianza excesiva *nf* excessive bail

fiscal *nm* prosecutor
fiscalía *nf* prosecution
forzar *v* force
fraude *nm* fraud
fraude tributario *nm* tax evasion
fraudulento *adj* fraudulent
fuera de toda duda razonable *adv* beyond a
    reasonable doubt
fuerza *nf* force
fuerza excesiva *nf* excessive force
fuerza mortífera *nf* deadly force
fuga *nf* escape, flight
fugarse *v* escape
fugitivo *nm* fugitive
fundamento suficiente *nm* reasonable basis
garantía de audiencia *nf* right to trial
garantía para fianza *nf* collateral for bail
grabación de investigación *nf* surveillance recording
grabación de vigilancia *nf* wiretap recording
guardia *nm* prison guard
habeas corpus *n* habeas corpus
hampa *nf* underworld
huellas digitales, huellas dactilares *nf* fingerprints
huida *nf* flight, escape
huir *v* flee
hurto *nm* larceny
hurto en tiendas *nm* shoplifting
hurto mayor *nm* grand larceny
imponer pena *v* sentence
imposibilidad *nf* impossibility
improcedente *(prueba)* *adj* inadmissible *(evidence)*

Criminal Law

imprudencia temeraria *nf* recklessness
impugnar una decisión *v* challenge a decision
impulso irresistible *nm* irresistible impulse
impune *adj* unpunished
inadmisible en los EE UU *adj* inadmissible to the U.S.
incautar *v* seize, confiscate, impound
incautarse la fianza *v* forfeit bail
incesto *nm* incest
inculpado *adj/n* accused
indocumentado *adj* undocumented
indulgencia *nf* leniency
indulgente *adj* lenient
indulto *nm* pardon
infancia *nf* infancy
informador *nm* informer
informante *nm* informant
informar *v* inform, tip off
informe acusatorio *nm* information
infracción *nf* infraction
infractor *nm* offender
inmunidad calificada *nf* qualified immunity
inocencia *nf* innocence
inocente *adj* innocent
intención *nf* intent
intención específica *nf* specific intent
intención general *nf* general intent
intencionalmente *adv* intentionally
intentar *v* attempt
intento *nm* attempt
interceptar *v* intercept
internamiento *nm* confinement

internar *v* confine, imprison
intervención de comunicación privada *nf* intercept
intoxicación *nf* intoxication
investigación *nf* investigation
investigador *nm* investigator
investigar *v* investigate
juegos de azar *nm* gambling
juegos de envite *nm* gambling
junta de libertad vigilada *nf* parole board
jurado *nm* juror, jury; *adj* sworn
jurado de acusación *nm* grand jury
jurado en desacuerdo *nm* hung jury
jurado indagatorio *nm* grand jury
juramentado *adj* sworn
juramento *nm* oath
jurar *v* swear
ladrón *nm* thief
ladrón ratero *nm* petty thief, shoplifter
lavado de dinero *nm* money laundering
lenidad *nf* leniency
lenocinio *nm* solicitation, pandering, pimping
lesiones graves *nf* serious bodily injury
lesivo *adj* prejudicial, harmful
ley *nf* law, statute
ley de expiración *nf* statute of limitations
ley de prescripción *nf* statute of limitations
liberado *adj* released, freed, discharged
liberar bajo fianza *v* release on bail
libertad condicional *nf* probation
libertad probatoria *nf* probation
libertad supervisada *nf* parole, conditional release

mala conducta *nf* misconduct
mala intención *nf* malice
malicia *nf* malice
maliciosamente *adv* maliciously
malicioso *adj* malicious
maltrato *nm* ill-treatment
malversación *nf* embezzlement
mara *nf* gang
marero *nm* gang member, gangster
mechero de tiendas *nm* shoplifter
métodos policíacos *nm* law enforcement methods
miedo *nm* fear
minoridad *nf* infancy
morgue *nf* morgue
motivo de acusación *nm* count of indictment
motivo fundado para sospechar *nm* probable cause
necesidad (defensa de) *nf* necessity *(defense of)*
negligencia dolosa *nf* criminal negligence
no corroborado *adj* uncorroborated
no culpable *adj* not guilty
nueva sentencia *nf* re-sentencing
obstrucción de la acción judicial *nf* obstruction
    of justice
oficial de libertad vigilada *nm* parole officer
operativo encubierto *nm* undercover operation
orden de allanamiento *nm* search warrant
orden de comparecencia *nf* summons, subpoena
orden de detención *nf* arrest warrant
orden de encarcelamiento *nf* commitment order
orden de remisión *nf* remanding order
orden de revisión *nf* search warrant

pagar la fianza *v* post bail
palpar *v* frisk
pandilla *nf* gang
pandillero *nm* gang member, gangster
partícipe *nm* accessory
pasar a juicio *v* go to trial
pasar el dato *v* tip off
pelea *nf* fight
pelear *v* fight
pena *nf* penalty, sentence, punishment
pena capital *nf* capital punishment, death penalty
pena concurrente *nf* concurrent sentence
pena consecutiva *nf* consecutive sentence
pena de muerte *nf* death penalty, capital punishment
pena indeterminada *nf* indeterminate sentence
pena intermitente *nf* intermittent sentence
pena leve *nf* light sentence
pena mínima obligatoria *nf* mandatory minimum
    sentence
pena simultánea *nf* concurrent sentence
pena sucesiva *nf* consecutive sentence
penal *adj* penal
penitenciaria *nf* penitentiary
período de encarcelamiento *nm* time in prison
perpetrador *nm* perpetrator
petición después del juicio *nf* motion after trial
petición para limitar la utilización de la prueba *nf*
    motion to limit the use of evidence
petición para suprimir pruebas *nf* motion to suppress
    evidence
pistola *nf* gun

Criminal Law

pistolero *nm* gunman

posesión *nf* possession

programa para protección de testigos *nm* witness protection plan

preacuerdo *nm* plea agreement, plea bargain

precedente *nm* precedent

premeditado *adj* premeditated

preponderancia de las pruebas *nf* preponderance of the evidence

presidio *nm* prison, penitentiary

preso *nm* prisoner, inmate

presunción *nf* presumption

presunción de inocencia *nf* presumption of innocence

presunción rebatible *nf* rebuttable presumption

presunción refutable *nf* rebuttable presumption

primera infracción *nf* first offense

prisión *nf* prison

prisionero *nm* prisoner

procedimiento disciplinario *nm* disciplinary proceedings

procesar *v* try, prosecute

prófugo *nm* fugitive

prohibido *adj* prohibited

prohibir *v* prohibit

prostitución *nf* prostitution

prostituta *nf* prostitute

proxeneta *nm* procurer, pimp

proxenetismo *nm* solicitation, pandering, pimping

prueba circunstancial *nf* circumstantial evidence

prueba exculpatoria *nf* exculpatory evidence

prueba eximente *nf* exculpatory evidence

prueba improcedent *nf* inadmissible evidence
prueba independiente *nf* independent evidence
prueba indirecta *nf* circumstantial evidence
pruebas insuficientes *nf* insufficient evidence
punitivo *adj* punitive
punto de acusación *nm* charge, count of indictment
purgar sentencia *v* serve a sentence
rapto *(de menores)* *nm* abduction, kidnapping *(of a minor)*
raptor *nm* abductor, kidnapper
reclusión perpetua *nf* life sentence
recluso *nm* inmate
recusación *nf* recusal, disqualification, challenge
recusación perentoria *(de jurado)* *nf* peremptory challenge *(of juror)*
recusación preventiva *(de jurado)* *nf* peremptory challenge *(of juror)*
recusación sin causa *(de jurado)* *nf* peremptory challenge *(of juror)*
redada *nf* dragnet
reformatorio *nm* reformatory
registro e incautación *nm* search and seizure
rehén *nm* hostage
reincidente *nm* recidivist, repeat offender
remisión de la duración de la pena por buen comportamiento *nf* good behavior time
remisión del proceso *nf* transfer of proceedings
rendición voluntaria *nf* voluntary surrender
rendirse *v* surrender, give up
renunciación *nf* renunciation
reo *nm* convict

reparación *nf* reparation
rescate *nm* ransom
responsabilidad objetiva *nf* strict liability
restitución *nf* restitution
resumen del fallo *nm* abstract of judgment
retirarse de una conspiración *v* withdraw from a
    conspiracy
revisión *nf* search, review
revisión judicial *nf* judicial review
revisión sin mandamiento *nf* warrantless search
revocación *nf* revocation, reversal
riña *nf* fight, brawl
robar del bolsillo *v* pick a pocket
robo *nm* theft
robo con escalo *nm* burglary
robo de identidad *nm* identity theft
rueda de sospechosos *nf* lineup
sanción *nf* sanction, penalty
sanción no-carcelaria *nf* non-jail sentence, alternative
    sentence
sancionar *v* sanction
saqueo *nm* looting
secuestrador *nm* abductor, kidnapper
secuestrar *v* abduct, kidnap
secuestro *nm* abduction, kidnapping
secuestro de menores *nm* kidnapping
sentencia *nf* sentence
sentencia firme *nf* final sentence
sobornar *v* suborn, bribe
soborno *nm* bribe, bribery
sobreseimiento de los cargos *nm* dismissal of charges

solicitar *v* request, apply, petition
sospecha *nf* suspicion
sospechar *v* suspect
sospechoso *nm* suspect
supervisión electrónica *nf* electronic monitoring
suspender la ejecución de la sentencia *v* stay
    enforcement of the judgment
sustracción de menores *nm* kidnapping
temer *v* fear
temerariamente *adv* recklessly
temerario *adj* reckless
temor *nm* fear
tenencia *nf* possession, holding
tentativa *nf* attempt
terrorismo *nm* terrorism
testigo *nm* witness
testigo adverso *nm* adverse witness
testigo de cargo *nm* prosecution witness
testigo ocular *nm* eyewitness
tirar *v* shoot
tirar a matar *v* shoot to kill
toma de rehenes *nf* hostage taking
trabajos comunitarios *nm* community service
traficante *nm* trafficker, smuggler
traficante de estupefacientes *nm* drug trafficker,
    drug dealer
transgresor *nm* offender
trastorno *(físico o mental)* *nm* disorder *(physical
    or mental)*
tratamiento vejatorio *nm* ill-treatment, mistreatment
usura *nf* usury

vandalismo *nm* vandalism
víctima *nf* victim
víctima vulnerable *nf* vulnerable victim
vigilancia *nf* surveillance
vigilancia de persona liberada *nf* post-release
    supervision
vigilancia electrónica *nf* electronic surveillance
violación *nf* rape
violar *v* rape
vista incoatoria *nf* arraignment
vista para la exclusión de pruebas *nf* suppression
    hearing
vista para lograr fianza *nf* bail hearing
vista para lograr libertad bajo palabra *nf* parole
    hearing
vista para sentencia *nf* sentencing hearing
vista probatoria *nf* evidentiary hearing
vista relativa a la libertad condicional *nf* probation
    hearing
voluntariamente *adv* willfully
voluntario *adj* willful

Derecho Penal

DERECHO DE FAMILIA
FAMILY LAW

El **derecho de familia** abarca eventos y relaciones familiares tales como el **nacimiento** y el **matrimonio**, o su disolución (**separación** o **divorcio**), y establece normas para el **mantenimiento** de los **dependientes** y la protección de los **hijos**. Un **decreto** de divorcio puede contener disposiciones relativas a la **custodia** y a las **visitas** que rigen los derechos y deberes de los padres divorciados hacia los hijos menores. Existen también leyes que establecen los requisitos para el matrimonio, tales como el requisito de haber cumplido la **edad de contraer matrimonio**, y leyes que estipulan las condiciones para la **anulación** del matrimonio o para obtener el cumplimiento de un **acuerdo prematrimonial**.

abandono del domicilio conyugal *nm* abandonment of marital domicile
abandono implícito *nm* constructive abandonment
aborto *nm* abortion
aborto espontáneo *nm* miscarriage
abuela *nf* grandmother
abuelo *nm* grandfather
abuelos *nm* grandparents
abuso de cónyuge *nm* spousal abuse
acogida temporal *nm* foster care
acta de defunción *nf* death certificate

Family Law

acta de divorcio *nf* divorce decree
acta de matrimonio *nf* marriage certificate
acta de nacimiento *nm* birth certificate
acta definitiva de divorcio *nf* final decree of divorce
acuerdo de resolución matrimonial *nm* marital
    settlement agreement
acuerdo de separación *nm* separation agreement
acuerdo prematrimonial *nm* pre-nuptial agreement
administrador de patrimonio *nm* administrator
    of estate
ADN *nm* DNA
adolescente *adj* adolescent, teenage; *nm* adolescent,
    teenager
adopción *nf* adoption
adoptar *v* adopt
adoptivo *adj* adoptive
adulterio *nm* adultery
adúltero *nm* adulterer
albacea *nm* executor
alumbramiento *nm* childbirth
amante *nm* lover, paramour
anticonceptivo *nm* contraceptive
anulación de matrimonio *nf* annulment of marriage
asesoramiento matrimonial *nm* marriage counseling
asignación de derechos de manutención *nf*
    assignment of support rights
asignación de ingresos *nf* earnings assignment
beneficiario *nf* beneficiary
bien matrimonial *nm* marital asset
bienestar *nm* well-being
bienestar del hijo *nm* best interests of the child

bigamía *nf* bigamy
bígamo *nm* bigamist
boda *nf* wedding, marriage ceremony
capacidad *(de personas)* *nf* competency *(of persons)*
casado *adj* married
casamiento *nm* marriage
casarse *v* marry
causales de divorcio *nm* grounds for divorce
ceremonia matrimonial *nf* marriage ceremony
certificado de nacimiento *nm* birth certificate
certificado médico *nm* medical certificate
clase de crianza de niños *nf* parenting class
clínica de maternidad *nf* maternity ward
composición *nf* settlement
condón *nm* condom
condonación *nf* condonation
consanguinidad *nm* consanguinity
consejero *nm* counselor
consejero matrimonial *nm* marriage counselor
consejo matrimonial *nm* marriage counseling
consejos *nm* guidance, advice
consentimiento *nm* consent
consentir *v* consent
contracepción *nf* contraception, birth control
contraer nuevas nupcias *v* remarry
cónyuge *nm* spouse
cónyuge putativo *nm* putative spouse
crédito tributario de adopción *nm* adoption tax credit
crueldad *nf* cruelty
cuidado de crianza *nm* foster care
cuñada *nf* sister-in-law

Family Law

cuñado *nm* brother-in-law
cuota alimentaria *nf* maintenance
curador *nm* guardian
curador ad litem *nm* guardian ad litem
custodia *nf* custody
custodia compartida *nf* shared custody
custodia conjunta *nf* joint custody
custodia exclusiva *nf* sole custody
custodia física *nf* physical custody
custodia legal *nf* legal custody
custodia temporal *nf* temporary custody
custodia única *nf* sole custody
deber de mantenimiento *nm* duty to support
declaraciones fraudulentas *nf* false pretenses
dependiente *adj/nm* dependent
derecho de familia *nm* family law
derechos de visita *(de los hijos por padre separado)*
    nm visitation rights *(of children by a separated*
    parent)
desavenencias *nf* irreconcilable differences
descendencia *nf* offspring, progeny
descuido *(de niño)* *nm* neglect *(of child)*
difunto *adj* deceased; *nm* deceased, decedent
disolución matrimonial *nf* dissolution of marriage
divorciado(a) *adj* divorced; *nm(f)* divorcee
divorciar *v* divorce
divorcio *nm* divorce
divorcio administrativo *nm* uncontested divorce
divorcio en firme *nm* absolute divorce
divorcio sin falta *nm* no-fault divorce
divorcio voluntario *nm* uncontested divorce

doméstico *adj* domestic
edad de contraer matrimonio *nm* marriageable age
emancipar *v* emancipate
embarazada *adj* expectant, pregnant
embarazo *nm* pregnancy
encinta *adj* pregnant
esponsales *nm* engagement *(to marry)*
esposa *nf* wife
esposo *nm* husband
ex-esposa *nf* ex-wife
ex-esposo *nm* ex-husband
fallecido *adj* deceased; *nm* deceased, decedent
familia *nf* family
familiar *nm* relative
fecundación artificial *nf* artificial insemination
fecundación in vitro *nf* in vitro fertilization
fecundo *adj* fertile
fidelidad *nf* fidelity
fiel *adj* faithful
finado *adj* deceased; *nm* deceased, decedent
formalizar *(matrimonio)* *v* solemnize *(marriage)*
gemelos *nm* twins
guardería *nf* child-care center, nursery
hermana *nf* sister
hermano *nm* brother
hermanos *nm* siblings
hija *nf* daughter
hijo *nm* son
hogar *nm* home
homosexual *adj/nm* homosexual
huérfano *nm* orphan

Family Law

ilegítimo *adj* illegitimate
impedimento a casarse *nm* impediment to marriage
impotencia *nf* impotence
impotente *adj* impotent
impuesto sobre donaciones *nm* gift tax
impuesto sucesorio *nm* estate tax
incapacitado *adj* incapacitated
incapaz *adj* incompetent
infecundidad *nf* sterility
infértil *adj* infertile
infertilidad *nf* infertility
infidelidad *nf* infidelity
infiel *adj* unfaithful
inseminación artificial *nf* artificial insemination
jefe de familia *nm* head of household
jubilación *nf* retirement
juez de lo familiar *nm* family court judge
juicio de paternidad *nm* paternity suit
juicio sucesorio *nm* surrogate court proceeding
juvenil *adj* juvenile
legítimo *adj* legitimate
lesbiana *nf* lesbian
licencia de maternidad *nf* maternity leave
madrastra *nm* stepmother
madre *nf* mother
madre portadora *nf* surrogate mother
maltrato del cónyuge *nm* spousal abuse
mantenimiento *nm* maintenance, support
mantenimiento del cónyuge *nm* spousal support
marido *nm* husband
maternidad *nf* maternity, motherhood

matrimonial *adj* matrimonial
matrimonio *nm* matrimony, marriage, married couple
matrimonio contraído en el extranjero *nm* foreign marriage
matrimonio homosexual *nm* gay marriage
mellizos *nm* twins
menor *adj* minor
menor de edad *adj* underage
menor emancipado *nm* emancipated minor
nacer *v* to be born
nacido muerto *adj* stillborn
nacimiento *nm* birth
nacimiento prematuro *nm* premature birth
nieta *nf* granddaughter
nieto *nm* grandchild
niño *nm* child
nodriza *nf* wet-nurse
novia *nf* fiancée
novio *nm* fiancé
nuera *nf* daughter-in-law
orden de retención de ingresos *nf* earnings withholding order
orden temporal *nm* temporary order
padrastro *nm* stepfather
padre *nm* father
padre biológico *nm* biological parent
padre con custodia *nm* custodial parent
padre con tutela *nm* custodial parent
padre de acogida *nm* foster parent
padre natural *nm* biological parent
padre putativo *nm* putative father

Family Law

padres *nm* parents
pareja *nf* couple
parentesco *nm* kinship
parientes políticos *nm* in-laws
partera *nf* midwife
parto *nm* childbirth
paternidad *nm* paternity
patrimonio *(del difunto)* *nm* estate *(of decedent)*
pautas *nf* guidelines
pensión alimentaria *nf* alimony, support
período de espera *(antes de declararse el divorcio)*
    nm waiting period *(for divorce)*
planificación familiar *nf* family planning
preservativo *nm* condom
primo *nm* cousin
progenie *nf* offspring, progeny
propiedad en común *nf* community property
propiedad individual *nf* separate property
propiedad matrimonial *nf* marital property
propiedad separada *nf* separate property
pubertad *nf* puberty
reconciliación *nf* reconciliation
reconocer *(hijo)* *v* recognize *(child)*
relaciones familiares *nf* domestic relations
remedio *nm* remedy, relief
retención *nf* garnishment, withholding
retención de ingresos *nf* income withholding
retención de sueldo *nf* wage withholding
reunificación familiar *nf* family reunification
separación legal *nf* legal separation
separación real *nf* actual separation

separado *adj* separated
sin testamento *adj* intestate
sobrina *nf* niece
sobrino *nm* nephew
socio doméstico *nm* domestic partner
solemnizar *(matrimonio)* *v* solemnize *(marriage)*
soltero *adj* single, unmarried
sostenimiento *nm* maintenance, support
suegra *nf* mother-in-law
suegro *nm* father-in-law
terapia *nf* therapy, counseling
tía *nf* aunt
tío *nm* uncle
transacción *nf* settlement
tribunal de familia *nm* family court
tutela *nf* guardianship, custody
tutor ad litem *nm* guardian ad litem
violencia doméstica *nf* domestic violence
violencia familiar *nf* domestic violence
visita *(de hijos por padre separado)* *nf* visitation *(of children by separated parent)*
viuda *nf* widow
viudo *nm* widower
vivir aparte y separados *v* live separate and apart
yerno *nm* son-in-law

Family Law

DERECHO DE SALUD
HEALTH-CARE LAW

El **derecho de salud** tiene que ver con las **lesiones**, las **enfermedades** y otras condiciones médicas que requieren **tratamiento** médico, la obtención de cobertura de **seguro** para tales tratamientos según los planes públicos y privados, y los requisitos establecidos para **ejercer** la profesión de médico y para la venta de **medicinas,** con vistas a proteger al público contra los riesgos a la salud y contra la **mala praxis**.

abondado *nm* subscriber
acceso *nm* access
acceso gratuito *nm* free access
acceso legal *nm* legal access
accidente *nm* accident
adicción *nf* addiction
agudo *adj* acute
aliviar *v* cure
aliviarse *v* get well
ambulatorio *adj* ambulatory
amenaza mortal *adj* life-threatening
amigdalas *nf* tonsils
amigdalitis *nf* tonsilitis
anciano *adj/nm* elder, senior citizen, elderly
anteojos *nm* eyeglasses
apendicitis *nm* appendicitis

aptitud física *nf* physical fitness
apto *adj* suited, apt, eligible
asbesto *nm* asbestos
asegurado *nm* insured, policyholder
asignación *nf* allowance
atención *nf* care
atención cardiológica *nf* cardiac care
atención de enfermería *nm* nursing care
atención de enfermería a domicilio *nf* at-home
    nursing care
atención inadecuada *nf* substandard care
atención integrada *nf* managed care
atención médica *nf* health care
atención médica contra el cáncer *nf* cancer care
auxiliar de casa *nm* home attendant
aviso de reclamo *nm* notice of claim
aviso de reclamo por escrito *nm* written notice
    of claim
beneficiario *nm* beneficiary
beneficio *nm* benefit
beneficio cubierto *nm* covered benefit
bienestar *nm* welfare
botiquín de primeros auxilios *nm* first-aid kit
calidad de vida *nf* quality of life
cáncer *nm* cancer
carcinógeno *nm* carcinogen
carie *nf* cavity
ceguera *nf* blindness
ciego según la pauta legal *adj* legally blind
cirugía *nf* surgery
cirujano *nm* surgeon

cita *nm* appointment
clínica *nf* clinic
cobertura *nf* coverage
cobertura adicional *nf* additional coverage
cobertura integral *nf* comprehensive coverage
cobertura para medicinas recetadas *nf* prescription
    drug coverage
compañía de seguro *nf* insurance company, insurer
compensación *nf* compensation
confiable *adj* dependable, reliable
consentimiento informado *nm* informed consent
consentir al tratamiento *v* consent to treatment
control de dolor *nm* pain management
control de peso *nm* weight management
co-pago *nm* co-payment
crónico *adj* chronic
cuidado *nm* care
cuidado adecuado *nm* adequate care
cuidado de ancianos *nm* elder care
cuidado intensivo *nm* acute care
cuidado preventivo *nm* preventive services
cuidador *nm* caregiver
cumplir con *v* satisfy, meet, comply with
cura *nf* cure
curandero *nm* healer
curar *v* cure
deductible *adj* deductible
denegar *v* deny
denegar tratamiento necesario *v* deny necessary
    treatment
dental *adj* dental

dentista *nm* dentist
derecho de ancianos *nm* elder law
dermatólogo *nm* dermatologist
descuido *nm* neglect
desempleo *nm* unemployment
designación de beneficiario *nf* beneficiary designation
diabetes *nm* diabetes
directiva anticipada *nf* living will
discapacidad *nf* disability
discapacitado *adj* disabled
doctor *nm* doctor
dolencia *nf* illness
dolor *nm* pain
droga *nf* drug
elegible *adj* eligible
enfermedad *nf* disease
enfermedad contagiosa *nf* infectious disease
enfermedad crónica *nf* chronic disease
enfermedad de la infancia *nf* childhood disease
enfermedad sexualmente transmisible *nf* sexually
    transmitted disease
enfermera *nf* nurse
enfermo *adj* sick, ill
envejeciente *nm* elder, senior citizen
examen preventivo *nm* preventive screening
exclusión de la póliza *nf* exclusion policy
fractura *nf* fracture
geriatría *nf* geriatrics
gestión sanitaria *nf* health-care management
gozar de prestaciones *v* to be entitled to benefits
gratuito *adj* free

hipertensión *nf* hypertension
hogar de ancianos *nm* nursing home
hospicio para ancianos *nm* nursing home
hospital *nm* hospital
hospitalizado *adj* hospitalized
impotencia *nf* impotence
incapacidad *nf* disability, handicap
incapacidad física *nf* physical disability
incapacidad mental *nf* mental disability
incapacidad temporal *nf* temporary disability
infección *nf* infection
invalidez permanente *nf* permanent disability
invalidez total permanente *nf* permanent total disability
legalmente incapacitado *adj* legally incapacitated
lentes de contacto *nm* contact lenses
lesión *nf* injury
lesión corporal *nf* physical injury
límite de la póliza *nm* policy limit
línea de referencia *nf* referral line
lisiado *adj* disabled
mal *nm* illness
mala praxis *nf* malpractice
medicamentos con receta médica *nm* prescription drugs
Medicare *n* Medicare
medicina *nf* medicine
medicina no tradicional *nf* non-traditional medicine
medicina preventiva *nf* preventive medicine
medicina tradicional *nf* traditional medicine
médico *adj* medical; *nm* doctor, physician
médico de familia *nm* family doctor
médico general *nm* general practitioner

mental *adj* mental

mudo *adj/nm* mute

negligencia profesional *nf* malpractice

norma *nf* standard

nutrición *nf* nutrition

obesidad *nf* obesity

optometrista *nm* optometrist

paciente externo *nm* out-patient

pago del reclamo *nm* payment of claim

pauta *nf* standard

pautas mínimas *nf* minimum standards

pérdida *nf* loss

pérdida de ambas manos y ambos pies *nf* loss of both hands and feet

pérdida de peso *nf* weight loss

pérdida de vida *nf* loss of life

pérdida del habla *nf* loss of speech

pérdida del oido *nf* loss of hearing

pérdida del pulgar y del índice de la misma mano *nf* loss of thumb and index finger of the same hand

pérdida total de la vista *nf* loss of entire sight

pericia *nf* expertise

peso *nm* weight

piedra nefrítica *nf* kidney stone

pintura a base de plomo *nf* lead paint

plan *nm* plan

poder de atención médica *nm* health-care proxy

póliza *nf* policy

póliza de seguro *nf* insurance policy

prestación *nf* benefit, service

prestación de acuerdo con la póliza *nf* policy benefit
prestación por seguro de discapacidad *nf* disability benefit
prevención *nf* prevention
prevención de enfermedades *nf* disease prevention
prevenir *v* prevent
preventivo *adj* preventive
prima de seguro *nf* insurance premium
probar *v* test
procedimiento de apelación *nm* appeal process
profesional *adj/nm* professional
proveedor *nm* provider
prueba *nf* test
prueba de pérdida *nf* proof of loss
psiquiatra *nm* psychiatrist
psiquiatría *nf* psychiatry
queja *nf* grievance, complaint
quemadura *nf* burn
quirófano *nm* operating room
receta médica *nf* prescription
rechazo *nm* denial
reclamación *nf* claim, grievance
reclamar *v* claim
reclamo *nm* claim
reclamo pendiente *nm* pending claim
reclamo por negligencia profesional *nm* malpractice claim
recuperación *nf* recovery
recuperar *v* recover
referencia *nf* referral
rehabilitación *nf* rehabilitation

relación proveedor-paciente *nf* provider-patient
    relationship
remedio *nm* remedy
renunciar a *v* waive
resistente a las drogas *adj* drug-resistant
retardo mental *nf* mental retardation
revisión de uso *nf* utilization review
riesgo excluido *nm* excluded risk
riñón *nm* kidney
sala de emergencias *nf* emergency room
sala de operaciones *nf* operating room
sala de recuperación *nf* recovery room
salud *nf* health
salud conductual *nf* behavioral health
salud del comportamiento *nf* behavioral health
salud laboral *nf* occupational health
salud mental *nf* mental health
salud prenatal *nf* prenatal health
saludable *adj* healthy
satisfacer *v* satisfy, meet, comply with
seguro *nm* insurance
seguro de recorrido *nm* common carrier coverage
seguro privado *nm* private insurance
servicio *nm* service
servicio amparado *nm* covered benefit, covered service
servicio cubierto *nm* covered benefit, covered service
servicio de referencia *nm* referral service
servicios de fertilidad *nm* fertility services
servicios diurnos para adultos *nm* adult day services
servicios para personas mayores *nm* senior services
servicios sociales *nm* social services

sistema de compensación *nm* compensation system
sobreviviente *nm* survivor
sordo *adj* deaf
sordomudo *adj/nm* deaf-mute
subscriptor *nm* subscriber
substancia controlada *nf* controlled substance
tener derecho a prestaciones *v* to be entitled to benefits
terapia *nf* therapy
terapia de conducto *nf* root canal therapy
terapia física *nf* physical therapy
testimonio *nm* will
titular de una póliza de seguro *nm* policyholder
tonsilas *nf* tonsils
tóxico *adj* toxic
tratamiento *nm* treatment
tratamiento de conducto *nf* root canal therapy
tratamiento médico necesario *nm* medically necessary
    treatment
tratar *v* treat
venda *nf* bandage
violencia doméstica *nf* domestic violence
vivienda asistida *nf* assisted living
vivir *v* live
vivo *adj* alive, living

DERECHO DE VIVIENDA
HOUSING LAW

El **derecho de vivienda** abarca las normas que rigen la **propiedad inmobiliaria**, el uso y **manetnimiento** de unidades de **vivienda** tales como los apartamentos, los contratos de **locación**, los **arrendamientos**, la **hipotecas**, y los derechos y deberes de los **propietarios** y los inquilinos. En los Estados Unidos, la mayoría de las cuestiones relativas a la vivienda se rigen por leyes estatales y locales.

abandonar *v* abandon
abandono de local *nm* abandonment of premises
acceso al local *nm* access to premises
accesorio *adj* accessory
acreedor hipotecario *nm* mortgagee
agente de bienes raíces *nm* real estate agent, realtor
albergue *nm* shelter
alojamiento *nm* housing
apartamento accesorio *nm* accessory apartment
arrendador *nm* lessor, landlord
arrendamiento *nm* lease
arrendamiento comercial *nm* commercial lease
arrendamiento de terreno *nf* ground lease
arrendar *v* lease
arrendatario *nm* lessee
ascensor *nm* elevator, lift

avalúo *nm* appraisal

aviso de desalojo *nm* notice to quit, notice of eviction

azotea *nf* terraced roof

bienes raíces *nm* real estate

calefacción *nf* heating

casa *nf* house

ceder posesión *v* vacate premises

cerca *nf* fence

cesión de arrendamiento *nf* assignment of lease

cláusula de caducidad de plazos *nf* acceleration clause

cláusula de prepago *nf* prepayment clause

concesión *nf* grant

construir *v* build

constructor *nm* builder

contrato de arrendamiento *nm* lease agreement

costos directos *nm* direct costs

depósito *nm* deposit

depósito de garantía *nm* security deposit

desalojar *v* evict

desalojo *nm* eviction

desalojo por orden judicial *nm* court-ordered eviction

desalojo presunto *nm* constructive eviction

desgaste de un bien *nm* wear and tear

desocupar *v* vacate premises

deterioro de un inmueble *nm* waste

deudor hipotecario *nm* mortgagor

donante *nm* grantor

donatario *nm* grantee

edificio *nm* building

ejecución hipotecaria *nf* foreclosure

ejecutar *(hipoteca)* v foreclose *(mortgage)*
elementos comunes *nm* common elements
elementos muebles adheridos *nm* fixtures
entrada ilegal a un inmueble ajeno *nf* trespass
escalera *nf* stair, stairway
escritura de donación *nf* deed of gift
escritura de fideicomiso *nf* deed of trust
escritura de propiedad *nf* deed
escritura mediante acto judicial *nf* judicial deed
escritura por cesión *nf* cession deed
estabilización de rentas *nf* rent stabilization
goce pacífico *nm* quiet enjoyment
gravamen *nm* lien
habitable *adj* habitable
hipoteca *nf* mortgage
hipoteca de pago global acelerado *nf* balloon mortgage
hipoteca de tasa ajustable *nf* adjustable rate
    mortgage (ARM)
hipoteca secundaria *nf* secondary mortgage
hipoteca subordinada *nf* junior mortgage
impuesto sobre la propiedad inmobiliaria *nm*
    property tax
inhabitable *adj* uninhabitable
inmueble *nm* building, real property
inquilino *nm* tenant
instalación *nf* fixture
litispendencia *nf* lis pendens
locatario *nm* tenant, renter, lessee
lote *nm* lot
mampara *nf* partition
mantener v maintain

Housing Law

mantenimiento *nm* maintenance

mercado de hipotecas secundarias *nm* secondary mortgage market

mercado residencial *nm* residential market

método de valuación según costos *nm* cost approach

ocupación *nf* occupancy

opción de prorrogar *nf* option to renew

pared *nf* wall

pared común *nf* party wall

pared medianera *nf* party wall

partición *nf* partition

patrimonio *nm* estate

permiso *nm* permit

permiso de uso especial *nm* special use permit

piso *nm* floor

plazo de arrendamiento *nm* lease term

posesión *nf* possession

precarista *nm* squatter

prescripción adquisitiva *nf* adverse possession

préstamo hipotecario *nm* mortgage loan

propiedad *nf* property, estate

propiedad residencial *nf* residential property

propiedad vitalicia *nf* life estate

propietario *nm* owner

puerta *nf* door

puntos *nm* points

ratificación *nf* ratification

razón de préstamo a valor *nf* loan-to-value ratio

redención *nf* redemption

redimir *v* redeem

régimen de control de rentas *nm* rent control

renta *nf* rent
renta básica *nf* base rent
rentar *v* rent
rescatar *v* redeem
rescate *nm* redemption
residencia *nf* residence
residencia principal *nf* principal residence
residencial *adj* residential
residente *nm* resident
retomar posesión *v* repossess
reversión *nf* reversion
revocación *nf* revocation
servicios urbanos *nm* utilities
servidumbre *nf* easement
sociedad constructora *nf* construction company
solar *nm* lot
subarrendar *v* sublease, sublet
subarrendatario *nm* sublessee, subtenant
subarriendo *nm* sublease, sublet
sublocación *nf* sublease, sublet
sublocatario *nm* sublessee, subtenant
techo *nm* roof
tenedor de un inmueble *nm* tenant
tenencia *nf* tenancy, occupancy
transferir *v* transfer, convey
tribunal de vivienda *nm* housing court
unidad de viviendas multifamiliar *nf* multi-family
    housing
urbanización *nf* housing project
uso accesorio *nm* accessory use
valor asegurado *nm* insured value

Housing Law

valor de mercado *nm* market value
valor de tasación *nm* assessed value
valoración *nf* valuation, appraisal
valuación *nf* valuation, appraisal
valla *nf* fence
vencimiento de arrendamiento *nm* expiration of
    lease term
ventana *nf* window
vitrina *nf* show-window
vivienda *nf* housing
vivienda con subsidio *nf* subsidized housing,
    low-income housing
vivienda justa *nf* fair housing
vivienda unifamiliar *nf* single-family home

◀

DERECHO MIGRATORIO
IMMIGRATION LAW

El **derecho migratorio** tiene que ver con las condiciones
para admitir a los Estados Unidos personas **extranjeras**
que ingresan ya sea de **visita** ya sea con el propósito de
hacerse **residentes** o **ciudadanos**. Las cuestiones migratorias quedan ahora bajo la autoridad del Department
of Homeland Security (Departamento de Seguridad
Nacional).

*Nota: Las cifras en paréntesis se refieren a formulatios
oficiales de los Estados Unidos.*

abogado de inmigración *nm* immigration lawyer
acta del procedimiento *nf* record of proceeding (ROP)
actividad terrorista *nf* terrorist activity
actual *adj* current
admisión *(al país)* *nf* admission *(to country)*
admisión autorizada de refugiado *nf* refugee
    authorized admission
admitido condicionalmente *nm* parolee
admitir a alguien condicionalmente a los EE UU *v*
    parole someone into the U.S.
afiliación *nf* affiliation
afirmación *nf* affirmation
agente de inmigración *nm* immigration officer
ajustar *(estado migratorio)* *v* adjust *(immigration status)*

Immigration Law

ajuste de estado migratorio *nm* adjustment of status

anulación de traslado *nf* cancellation of removal

anulación provisional *nf* cancellation without
    prejudice

apátrida *adj* stateless

aplazamiento de deportación *nf* withholding of
    deportation

aplazamiento del traslado *nm* withholding of removal

aprobación del estado de refugiado *nf* refugee
    approval

archivo central de direcciones *nm* central address file

archivo de inmigración *nm* immigration record

asilado *nm* asylee

asilo *nm* asylum

asilo político *nm* political asylum

atestación *nf* attestation, certificate

atribución *(de país de origen)* *nf* charge *(as to country
    of origin)*

audiencia de redeterminación de custodia *nf*
    custody redetermination hearing

audiencia de traslado forzoso *nf* removal hearing

audiencia sin demora *nf* expedited hearing

autorización de empleo *nf* employment authorization

**aviso al extranjero detenido de la audiencia
    de exclusión** *nm* notice to alien detained for
    exclusion hearing (I-122)

aviso de aprobación *nm* approval notice

aviso de audiencia de asilo solamente *nm* notice of
    asylum-only hearing

aviso de audiencia de deportación *nm* notice of
    deportation hearing

aviso de audiencia de traslado forzoso *nm* notice of
removal hearing

**aviso de comparecer en el procedimiento de
traslado forzoso** *nm* notice to appear for removal
proceedings

aviso de derechos *nm* advisal of rights

**aviso de intención de expedir una orden
administrativa final de deportación** *nm*
notice of intent to issue a final administrative
deportation order (I-851)

**aviso de intención de rescindir y petición de
audiencia por parte del extranjero** *nm* notice
of intention to rescind and request for hearing
by alien

aviso de las consecuencias por incomparecencia *nm*
notice of consequences for failure to appear

aviso de remisión a un juez de inmigración *nm*
notice of referral to immigration judge

aviso de revisión de la condición reclamada *nm*
notice of review of claimed status

**aviso del privilegio a recibir asistencia legal/
letrada** *nm* notice of privilege of counsel

**aviso sobre las consecuencias de no cumplir con la
orden de salida** *nm* notice of consequences for
failure to depart

**aviso sobre las consecuencias de presentar a
sabiendas una solicitud de asilo sin mérito** *nm*
notice of consequences for knowingly filing a
frivolous asylum application

beneficiario indirecto *nm* derivative beneficiary

cambio de condición *nm* change of status

carta de naturalización *nf* naturalization papers

categoría de llegada *nf* arrival category

categoría de preferencia *nf* preference category

caución de salida voluntaria *nf* voluntary departure bond

caución relacionada con la conservación de la condición y la salida *nf* maintenance of status and departure bond

centro de ayuda para solicitantes *nm* application support center

centro de servicio *nm* service center

ceremonia de juramento *nf* swearing-in ceremony

ceremonia de naturalización *nf* naturalization ceremony

certificación de trabajo a extranjeros *nf* alien labor certification

certificación laboral *nf* labor certification

certificado de ciudadanía *nm* certificate of citizenship

certificado de matrimonio *nm* marriage certificate

certificado de naturalización *nm* certificate of naturalization

circunstancias distintas *nf* changed circumstances

circunstancias excepcionales *nf* exceptional circumstances

ciudadanía *nf* citizenship

ciudadanía adquirida *nf* acquired citizenship

ciudadanía indirecta *nf* derivative citizenship

ciudadano naturalizado *nm* naturalized citizen

claramente y más allá de toda duda *adv* clearly and beyond a doubt

con derecho a ser admitido *adj* entitled to be admitted

condición actual *nf* current status
condición de asilado *nf* asylee status
condición de protección provisional *nf* temporary
    protected status
condición de refugiado *nf* refugee status
condición derivada *nf* derivative status
condición indirecta *nf* derivative status
consulado *nm* consulate
contrato declaración jurada de patrocinio
    económico entre el patrocinador y un miembro
    del hogar *nm* affidavit of support contract
    between sponsor and household member (I-864A)
Convención de las Naciones Unidas Contra la
    Tortura *nf* United Nations Convention against
    Torture
cónyuge golpeada(o) *nf(m)* battered spouse
cónyuge inmigrante maltratada(o) *nf(m)* abused
    immigrant spouse
cónyuge inmigrante víctima(o) de abuso *nf(m)*
    abused immigrant spouse
co-solicitante *nm* co-applicant
costo de tramitación *nm* filing fee
creíble dadas las condiciones del país *adj* plausible
    in light of country conditions
crimen particularmente grave *nm* particularly
    serious crime
crueldad extrema *nf* extreme cruelty
cruzafronteras *nm* border crosser
cuota *nf* quota
datos biográficos *nm* biographical information
decisión reservada *nf* reserved decision

Immigration Law

declaración jurada de apoyo económico *nf* affidavit
of support
declaración jurada de patrocinio económico *nf*
affidavit of support (I-864)
dependiente *nm/adj* dependent
deportación *nf* deportation
deportar *v* deport
detención obligatoria *nf* mandatory detention
discreción *nf* discretion
disposiciones especiales de naturalización *nf* special
naturalization provisions
documento justificante *nm* supporting document
domiciliado *adj* domiciled
domicilio *nm* domicile
dominio del inglés *nm* English proficiency
duración del estado o condición *nf* duration of status
elegibilidad *nf* eligibility
emigrante *nm* emigrant
empleo *nm* employment, occupation, job
entrevista *nf* interview
esposa golpeada *nf* battered wife
establecer el derecho a la condición de refugiado *v*
establish eligibility as a refugee
estadía no autorizada *nf* overstay, unlawful stay
estado civil *nm* marital status
estudiante *nm* student
estudiante a tiempo completo *nm* full-time student
excepción por motivos médicos *nf* medical waiver
exclusión *nf* exclusion
exención para esposa golpeada *nf* battered spouse
waiver

expulsar *v* expel, remove
expulsión *nf* expulsion
extensión de visa *nf* visa extension
extranjero *adj* foreign, alien, overseas; *nm* alien
extranjero admitido condicionalmente *nm* paroled alien
extranjero delincuente *nm* criminal alien
extranjero en tránsito *nm* transit alien
extranjero inadmisible *nm* inadmissible alien
extranjero legalizado *nm* legalized alien
extranjero o visitante por programa de intercambio *nm* exchange alien, exchange visitor
extranjero principal *nm* principal alien
extranjero que llega *nm* arriving alien
extranjero residente *nm* resident alien
extranjero residente permanente legal *nm* lawful permanent resident alien (LPRA)
extranjero sujeto a deportación *nm* deportable alien
extranjero sujeto a traslado forzoso *nm* removable alien
extranjero víctima de malos tratos *nm* abused alien
factor negativo *nm* negative factor
familiar acompañante *nm* accompanying relative
fecha *nf* date
fecha de llegada *nf* arrival date
fecha de prioridad *nf* priority date
fecha de registro *nf* registry date
fecha de vencimiento *nf* expiration date, cut-off date
firmemente restablecido *adj* firmly resettled
fraude matrimonial *nm* marriage fraud
fuera de estado *adj* out of status

Immigration Law

funcionario consular *nm* consular officer
funcionario encargado de las solicitudes de asilo *nm*
    asylum officer
golpeado(a) *adj* battered
habeas corpus *n* habeas corpus
idoneidad prima facie *nf* prima facie eligibility
impedimento a la readmisión *nm* bar to readmission
impedimento al asilo *nm* bar to asylum
inelegible *adj* ineligible
informe de inmigración *nm* immigration record
ingreso del hogar *nm* household income
inmediato familia o familiar *adj* immediate family
    or relative
inmigración *nm* immigration
inmigrante *nm* immigrant
inmigrante de preferencia *nm* preference immigrant
inmigrante especial *nm* special immigrant
interés nacional *nm* national interest
juez de inmigración *nm* immigration judge (IJ)
junta de admisión condicional *nf* parole board
Junta de Apelaciones de Inmigración *nf* Board of
    Immigration Appeals
juramento *nm* oath
laboratorio forense de documentos *nm* forensic
    document laboratory
legalmente admitido *adj* lawfully admitted
legitimado *adj* legitimated
libertad condicional *nf* parole
libertad condicional anticipada *nf* advance parole
límite anual *nm* annual limit

límite numérico *nm* numerical limit
límite por país *nm* per-country limit
llegada de refugiado *nf* refugee arrival
lotería *nf* lottery
lugar de la última entrada *nm* place of last entry
médico del panel *nm* panel physician
menor no acompañado *nm* unaccompanied minor
migrante *nm* migrant
migratorio *adj* immigration
nacionalidad *nf* nationality
naturalización *nf* naturalization
niño golpeado *nm* battered child
nivel de educación *nm* level of education, educational
    level
no divulgación *nf* non-disclosure
no inmigrante *nm* non-immigrant
notificación de audiencia de deportación *nm* notice
    of deportation hearing
**notificación de cambio de dirección del
    patrocinador** *nf* sponsor's notice of change of
    address (I-865)
notificación de intención de rescindir *nf* notice of
    intent to rescind
número de caso *nm* case number
numero de causa *nm* case number
numero de expediente *nm* case number
número de registro de extranjeros *nm* alien
    registration number
número de seguro social *nm* Social Security Number
    (SSN)
obstáculo de inmigración *nm* immigration hold

Immigration Law

oficina regional *nf* regional office
orden de salida voluntaria *nf* voluntary departure order
orden final de deportación *nf* final order of removal
orden reemplazante de traslado forzoso *nm* alternate
  order of removal
otorgamiento condicional *nm* conditional grant
país de nacimiento *nm* country of birth
paquete calendario de citas *nm* appointment
  package
paquete de instrucciones *nm* instruction package
pasaporte *nm* passport
pasaporte legible mecánicamente *nm* machine
  readable passport (MRP)
patrocinador *nm* sponsor
patrocinante *nm* sponsor
patrocinante conjunto *nm* joint sponsor
patrocinio *nm* sponsorship
patrulla fronteriza *nf* border patrol
peligro para la comunidad *nm* danger to the
  community
permiso de regresar al país *nm* re-entry permission
persecución económica *nf* economic persecution
persecución relacionada con el género *nf*
  gender-related persecution
persona indigente *nf* public charge
persona trasladada por la compañía *nf*
  intracompany transferee
petición de asilo *nf* asylee application
petición de inmigrante *nf* immigrant petition
petición de resolución *nf* motion for termination
petición de revisión *nf* petition for review

petición de un extranjero por compromiso matrimonial *nf* petition for alien fiance(e) (I-129F)

petición de un familiar extranjero *nf* petition for alien relative (I-130)

petición para clasificar a un huérfano como familiar inmediato *nf* petition to classify orphan as an immediate relative (I-600)

polizón *nm* stowaway

posibilidad significativa *nf* significant possibility

precluir *v* preclude

pre-inspección *nf* pre-inspection

presencia física continua *nf* continuous physical presence

presentarse para el traslado *v* surrender for removal

presente ilegalmente *adj* unlawfully present

privación extrema *nf* extreme hardship

procedimiento de traslado *nm* removal proceeding

procedimiento de traslado expedito *nm* expedited removal proceeding

proceso de asilo afirmativo *nm* affirmative asylum process

proceso de asilo defensivo *nm* defensive asylum process

profesión *nf* occupation, profession

profesión especializada *nf* specialty occupation

programa piloto de exención de visa *nm* visa waiver pilot program

prórroga de estadía *nf* extension of stay

próximo a convertirse en conviviente *adj* following to join

Immigration Law

prueba clara y convincente *nf* clear and convincing evidence

prueba inequívoca, clara y convincente *nf* clear, convincing and unequivocal evidence

puerto de entrada *nm* port of entry

reasentamiento *nm* resettlement

refugiado *nm* refugee

refugio seguro *nm* safe haven

regla de un año *nf* one-year rule

reglas de custodia del período de transición *nf* transitional period custody rules

relación familiar que confiere un derecho *nf* qualifying family relationship

reparación discrecional *nf* discretionary relief

reparación para el cónyuge/infante golpeado o maltratado *nf* battered spouse/child relief

repatriación *nf* removal, repatriation

residencia continua *nf* continuous residence

residencia legal permanente *nf* lawful permanent residence

residente condicional *nm* conditional resident

residente de retorno *nm* returning resident

residente permanente *nm* permanent resident

respuesta del Departamento de Estado *nf* State Department response

revisión de la condición *nf* status review

salida bajo supervisión *nf* departure under safeguards

salida obligatoria *nf* required departure

salida voluntaria *nf* voluntary departure

salida voluntaria al concluir el proceso *nf* voluntary departure at the conclusion of proceedings

salida voluntaria previa a la conclusión del proceso *nf* voluntary departure prior to completion of proceedings

sanciones por contumacia *nf* sanctions for contemptuous conduct

sector de la patrulla fronteriza *nm* Border Patrol Sector

sentencia diferida, suspendida *nf* deferred sentence

sin hogar *adj* homeless

sin techo *adj* homeless

Sistema de Preferencia *nm* Preference System

sistema nacional automatizado para la revisión de inmigración *nm* automated nationwide system for immigration review

solicitante *nm* applicant, petitioner

solicitante de admisión *nm* applicant for admission

solicitante de asilo *nm* asylum seeker

solicitar visa *v* apply for a visa

solicitud *nf* application

solicitud de asilo suplementaria *nf* supplemental asylum application

solicitud de autorización de empleo *nf* application for employment authorization (I-765)

solicitud de cambio de clasificación *nm* application for adjustment of status

solicitud de cancelación del traslado *nm* application for cancellation of removal

solicitud de certificado de ciudadanía *nm* application for certification of citizenship (N-600)

Immigration Law

solicitud de naturalización *nf* naturalization application

solicitud de reemplazo del documento de ciudadanía por naturalización *nf* application for replacement of naturalization citizenship document (N-565)

solicitud de renovación *nf* renewal application

solicitud de trámite adelantado para la petición de un huérfano *nm* application for advance processing of orphan petition (I-600A)

solicitud para registrar la residencia permanente o para cambiar el estado legal *nf* application to register permanent residence or to adjust status (I-485)

solicitud sin mérito *nf* frivolous application

sujeto a traslado forzoso *adj* removable

tarjeta de entrada-salida *nf* Arrival-Departure Card (I-94)

tarjeta de identificación *nf* identification card

tarjeta de residente permanente *nf* permanent resident card (PRC), alien registration receipt card (I-551)

tarjeta verde *nf* green card (I-551)

temor de persecución fundado *nm* well-founded fear of persecution

temor genuino de persecución *nm* genuine fear of persecution

tercer país seguro *nm* safe third country

tomar el juramento de quienes adquieren ciudadanía *v* swear in citizens

trabajador agrícola *nm* agricultural worker
trabajador agrícola especial *nm* special agricultural worker (SAW)
trabajador lego *nm* lay worker
trabajador temporal *nm* temporary worker
Tránsito sin Visa *nm* Transit Without Visa (TWOV)
trasladar *v* remove
trasladar a expensas del gobierno *v* remove at government expense
traslado (forzoso) *nm* removal
traslado por motivos penales *nm* criminal removal
tribunal de naturalización *nm* naturalization court
tripulante *nm* crew member
última residencia *nf* last residence
verificación de archivos *nf* records check
vileza moral *nf* moral turpitude
visa *nf* visa
visa A-1 *nf* A-1 visa
visa A-2 *nf* A-2 visa
visa A-3 *nf* A-3 visa
visa B-1 *nf* B-1 visa
visa B-1/B-2 *nf* B1/B2 visa
visa B-2 *nf* B-2 visa
visa de acompañante *nf* accompanying visa
visa de comerciante del tratado *nf* treaty trader visa
visa de inmigrante *nf* immigrant visa
visa de inversionista para países del tratado *nf* treaty investor visa
visa de no inmigrante *nf* non-immigrant visa
visa de residencia condicionada *nf* conditional residence visa

Immigration Law

visa legible por máquina *nf* machine-readable visa (MRV)

visa para novios con compromiso nupcial *nf* K-1 Visa, Fiancé(e) Visa

visitante de negocios no-inmigrante *nm* business non-immigrant

DERECHO DE TRÁNSITO
TRAFFIC LAW

El **derecho de tránsito** abarca las normas que rigen el
uso de los **vehículos motorizados** el las **vías** públicas,
los requisitos para obtener un **permiso de conducir**, los
requisitos relativos a los **seguros**, las penalidades por
incumplimieno a las reglas de tránsito, y los métodos de
hacer cumplir medidas de **seguridad** tales como el requisito de llevar **cinturón de seguridad** y la prohibición
de **conducir en estado de ebriedad**.

abandonar el lugar del accidente *v* leaving the scene
    of an accident
abrocharse el cinturón de seguridad *v* buckle up
accidental *adj* accidental
accidente *nm* accident
accidente fatal *nm* fatal accident
acera *nf* sidewalk
acumulación de puntos *nf* accumulation of points
**Administración Federal de Seguridad de Vehículos
    de Transporte** *nf* Federal Motor Carrier Safety
    Administration (FMCSA)
**Administración Nacional de Seguridad de
    Tránsito** *nf* Natonal Highway Traffic Safety
    Administration (NHTSA)
alcoholemia *nf* Blood Alcohol Concentration (BAC)
Alto Stop

Traffic Law

ambulancia *nf* ambulance

aparato detector de radar *nm* radar detector

aparcamiento de lado alternativo *nm* alternate-side parking

área de descanso *nf* rest area

asiento de seguridad *nm* child safety seat

atravesar una zona de seguridad *v* driving through a safety zone

atropellar *v* run down, run over

atropellar y huir *v* hit and run

audiencia *nf* hearing

autobus escolar *nm* school bus

automovilista *nm* motorist

automovilista con seguro insuficiente *nm* under-insured motorist (UIM)

automovilista sin seguro *nm* uninsured motorist (UM)

autopista *nf* expressway, freeway, turnpike

avenida *nf* avenue

aviso de anulación del permiso de conducir *nm* notice of revocation of driver's license

aviso de suspensión o anulación del permiso de conducir *nm* notice of suspension or revocation of driver's license

bebida alcohólica *nf* alcoholic beverage

bloquearle el paso a alguien *v* cut someone off

boleta de infracción *nf* ticket

borde de la carretera *nm* shoulder of the road

brocal *nm* curb

calcomanía de inspección *nf* inspection sticker

calle *n* street

calle de vía libre *nf* through street

calle transitada *nf* thoroughfare
cambiar de carril *v* change lanes
cambiar de carril de manera imprudente *v* make
    unsafe lane changes
camellón *nm* median strip
carretera *nf* road, highway
carril para vehículos de alta ocupación (VAO) *nm*
    high-occupancy vehicle (HOV) lane
ceder el paso *v* yield
cédula de seguro *nf* insurance identification card
chofer *nm* driver, chauffeur
choque *nm* crash
cinturón de seguridad *nm* seatbelt
código de tránsito *nm* vehicle code
colisión *nf* collision
colisión frontal *nf* head-on collision
colisión lateral *nf* side collision
colisión trasera *nf* rear-end collision
comprobante de seguro *nm* proof of insurance
Concentración de Alcohol en la Sangre (CAS) *nf*
    Blood Alcohol Concentration (BAC)
condena en rebeldía *nf* default conviction
condena por falta de comparecencia *nf* default
    conviction
conducción de vehículo sin licencia con
    circunstancias agravantes *nm* aggravated
    unlicensed operation (AUO)
conducción defensiva *nf* defensive driving
conducción imprudente *nm* reckless driving
conducción temeraria *nm* reckless driving

Traffic Law

conducir *v* drive

conducir bajo la influencia de alcohol o estupefacientes *v* driving under the influence of alcohol or drugs (DUI)

conducir con capacidad disminuída *v* driving while ability impaired (DWAI)

conducir con licencia suspendida *v* driving while license suspended

conducir con licencia vencida *v* driving with an expired license

conducir en estado de ebriedad *v* drunk driving

conducir en estado de intoxicación *v* driving while intoxicated (DWI)

conducir en sentido contrario al tráfico *v* moving against traffic

conducir sin cuidado *nm* careless driving

conductor *nm* driver

conductor sin la edad requerida para conducir *nm* underage driver

confiscar *(un vehículo)* *v* impound *(a vehicle)*

Conserve Su Derecha Keep Right

Conserve Su Izquierda Keep Left

correa de hombro *nf* shoulder harness

Cruce Crossroad

cruce para peatones *nm* crosswalk, pedestrian crossing

culebrear entre carriles *v* weave between lanes

curso de seguridad vial *nm* traffic safety school

curva *nf* curve

Curva Peligrosa Dangerous Curve

daño material *nm* property damage

dar vuelta *v* turn

dar vuelta incorrectamente ante un semáforo *v*
improper turn at traffic light

dar vuelta sin señalar *v* failure to use turn signals

Departamento de Transporte *nm* Department of
Transportation (DOT)

Departamento de Vehículos Motorizados *nm*
Department of Motor Vehicles (DMV)

derecha *adj/adv* right

deslizar *v* slide

desobediencia de señales de tráfico *nf* failure to obey
a traffic control device

despacio *adj/adv* slow

Desvío Detour

distancia de frenado *nf* braking distance

distancia de reacción *nf* reaction distance

emplazamiento *nm* citation, summons

encrucijada *(de autopista)* *nf* interchange *(highway)*

entregar licencia *v* turn in a license

escuela de manejo *nf* driving school

escuela para infractores de tráfico *nf* traffic violator
school

esquina *nf* corner

estacionamiento *nm* parking lot, parking garage

estacionamiento en batería *nm* parallel parking

estacionamiento en línea *nm* parallel parking

estacionar en doble fila *nm* double parking

exceder la velocidad máxima *v* exceeding maximum
speed limit

falta *nf* fault

falta de comparecencia *nf* failure to appear

fecha de comparecencia *nf* court appearance date

Traffic Law

Ferrocarril Railroad
frenar *v* brake
freno de emergencia *nm* emergency brake
frenos *nm* brakes
garage *nm* garage
gasolina *nf* gasoline
gasolinera *nf* gas station, filling station
historial de conductor sin tacha *nm* clean driving
    record
historial del conductor *nm* driver record
impacto *nm* impact
impacto frontal *nm* frontal impact
impugnar *v* contest, challenge
impugnar una boleta de infracción *v* challenge
    a ticket
inapropiado *adj* improper
incorrecto *adj* improper
incumplimiento de pago de la multa *nm* failure to
    pay fine (FTP)
informe de accidente *nm* accident report
informe policíaco *nm* police report
infracción *nf* violation, infraction
infracción de los reglamentos relativos a los seguros
    nf insurance violation
infracción de tránsito *nf* traffic violation, traffic ticket
infracción por conducir en estado de ebriedad *nf*
    drinking and driving offense
infracción por esperar en zona prohibida *nf*
    standing violation
infracción por exceso de velocidad *nf* speeding ticket

infracción por mal estacionamiento *nf* parking violation, parking ticket

infracción por no ceder el paso a un peaton en un cruce para peatones *nf* failure to yield to pedestrian in crosswalk

infracción por no ceder la prioridad de paso *nf* failure to yield right of way

infracción por no parar ante un semáforo *v* failure to stop at traffic light

infracción por pasar un autobus escolar parado *nf* passing of a stopped school bus

infracción por vehículo en mal estado *nf* fix-it ticket

infracción que no requiere comparecencia *nf* non-mandatory appearance violation

infracción que requiere comparecencia *nf* mandatory appearance violation, court appearance violation

infracción relativa a la condición mecánica del vehículo *nf* mechanical violation

infracción relativa al mal uso de los carriles *nf* lane violation

infracción sumaria *nf* summary offense

infractor *nm* violator

intoxicacón *nf* intoxication

isleta canalizadora *nf* gore zone, gore point

izquierda *adj* left

klaxon *nm* horn

lesión *nf* injury

letrero *nm* sign

licencia condicional *nf* conditional license

licencia confiscada *nf* confiscated license

licencia de conducir *nf* driver's license
licencia de conducir provisional *nf* provisional
    driver's license
límite de velocidad *nm* speed limit
límite de velocidad anunciado *nm* posted speed limit
limpiaparabrisas *nm* windshield wiper
llanta *nf* tire
llanta desinflada *nf* flat tire
llanta ponchada *nf* flat tire
lugar de un accidente *nm* scene of an accident
luz ámbar *nf* yellow light
luz intermitente *nf* flashing light
luz relampagueante *nf* flashing light
luz roja *nf* red light
luz verde *nf* green light
manejar *v* drive
**manejo de vehículo sin licencia con circunstancias
    agravantes** *nm* aggravated unlicensed
    operation (AUO)
manejo imprudente *nm* reckless driving
manejo temerario *nm* reckless driving
matrícula *nf* registration
matrícula de vehículo *nf* vehicle registration
moderar velocidad *v* reduce speed
motor *nm* motor
negligencia contribuyente *nf* contributory negligence
neumático *nf* tire
No Hay Salida Dead End/No Exit
obstculizar el tráfico *v* impede traffic
ocupantes del asiento delantero *nm* front-seat
    occupants

orden de comparecencia *(por una infracción)* nf
   citation, summons *(for an infraction)*
pagar por correo *v* pay by mail
parabrisas *nm* windshield
parada *nf* stop
parada de emergencia *nf* emergency stop
parar *v* stop
parquímetro *nm* parking meter
pasajero *nm* passenger
pasar a otro vehículo incorrectamente *v* pass
   improperly
pasar por alto un semáforo en rojo *v* run a red light
pasar por alto una señal de alto *v* run a stop sign
pasar por la derecha de otro vehículo *v* pass on
   the right
patrulla de carreteras *nf* highway patrol
peaje *nm* toll
peaton *nm* pedestrian
Peligro Danger
peligro *nm* danger, hazard
pérdida de privilegios de conductor *nf* loss of
   driving privileges
permiso de conducir digital *nm* digital driver license
   (DDL)
permiso de principiante *nm* learner's permit
placa *nf* license plate
Precaución Caution
prioridad de paso *nf* right of way
privilegio de conducir *nm* driving privilege
programa de permiso de conducir condicional *nm*
   probationary driver program

Traffic Law

programa para conductores alcohólicos *nm* drinking driver program (DDP)

programa para conductores con conducta agresiva *nm* aggressive driver program

programa para mejorar la conducción *nm* driver improvement program

Prohibido Estacionar No Parking

Prohibido Parar No Stopping

prueba de aliento *nf* breath test

prueba de identidad *nf* proof of identity

puente *nm* bridge

rebasar la velocidad máxima *v* exceed maximum speed limit

reducción de puntos *nf* reduction in points

reducir velocidad *v* reduce speed

reglas de tránsito *nf* rules of the road

responder a una boleta de infracción *v* answer a ticket

responsabilidad financiera *nf* financial responsibility

restablecimiento *nm* reinstatement, restoration

restricción *nf* restriction

reventón de llanta *nm* tire blowout

revocación *nf* revocation

rótulo *nm* sign

rueda *nf* wheel

salida de autopista *nf* off-ramp

segunda infracción *nf* second offense

seguridad vial *nf* road safety

seguro contra lesiones personales *nm* Personal Injury Protection (PIP)

seguro de responsabilidad personal *nm* liability
insurance
seguro para vehículo *nm* vehicle insurance
semáforo *nm* traffic light
señal de tránsito *nf* traffic sign
sentido único *adj* one-way
síndrome del latigazo *nm* whiplash
sirena *nf* siren
sistema de puntos *nm* point system
sonar el klaxon *v* honk
suspensión *nf* suspension
tarjeta de circulación vehicular *nf* registration card
tarjeta de seguro *nf* insurance identification card
tiempo de reacción *nm* reaction time
transacción de seguro *nf* insurance settlement
transmisión *nf* transmission
tribunal de infracciones de tráfico *nm* traffic court
uso ilegal de camellón *nm* unlawful use of median
strip
vehículo *nm* vehicle
vehículo confiscado *nm* impounded vehicle
vehículo desatendido *nm* unattended motor vehicle
vehículo motorizado *nm* motor vehicle
vehículo motorizado comercial *nm* commercial
motor vehicle (CMV)
vehículo sin seguro *nm* uninsured vehicle
vehículos de emergencia *nm* emergency vehicles
velocidad *nf* speed
vía pública *nf* thoroughfare
vista *nf* hearing

Traffic Law

volante *nm* steering wheel
volcar *v* overturn
volcarse *(un vehículo)* *v* roll over *(a vehicle)*
Zona Escolar School Zone

ENGLISH - SPANISH
INGLÉS – ESPAÑOL

GENERAL AND PROCEDURAL TERMS
TÉRMINOS GENERALES Y PROCESALES

abandon *v* abandonar
abandonment *n* abandono
abrogate *v* abrogar
abstract *(summary)* *n* resumen, extracto
abstract of judgment *n* resumen del fallo
abuse *n* abuso; *v* abusar
abuse of power *n* abuso de poder
abuse of trust *n* abuso de confianza
acknowledgment of satisfaction of judgment *n*
    reconocimiento de pago del fallo
action *(civil)* *n* demanda
ad litem *adj* ad litem, para el caso
addict *n* adicto
addiction *n* adicción
adjourn *v* suspender
adjourned *adj* suspendido
adjournment *n* suspensión
adjudicate *v* fallar, juzgar, resolver
adjudication *n* fallo, sentencia
adjuster *(insurance)* *n* liquidador, ajustador *(de
    seguros)*
administer *v* administrar
administration *n* administración, gobierno

administrative *adj* administrativo
administrator *n* administrador
admissible evidence *n* pruebas admisibles
admission *n* admisión
admonish *v* amonestar, advertir
admonition *n* amonestación, advertencia
adult *adj/n* adulto
adversarial system *n* sistema contencioso
adverse witness *n* testigo adverso
affair *n* asunto
affidavit *n* afidávit, declaración jurada por escrito
affirm *v* afirmar, confirmar, ratificar
affirmance *(of a decision)* *n* confirmación, ratificación
   (de una decisión)
affix signature *v* agregar firma
aggrieved party *n* persona perjudicada, persona
   agraviada
agreement *n* acuerdo, contrato, convenio
AIDS *n* SIDA (síndrome de inmunodeficiencia
   adquirida)
alcohol *n* alcohol
alcoholic *adj/n* alcohólico
alcoholism *n* alcoholismo
alien *adj/n* extranjero, foráneo
allegation *n* alegación, alegato, denuncia
allege *v* alegar, sostener
alter *v* alterar, modificar
alternate *adj* alterno
amend *v* enmendar
amendment *n* enmienda
amount *n* monto, suma, cantidad

amphetamine *n* anfetamina
annul *v* anular, declarar nulo
appeal *n* apelación, recurso; *v* apelar, recurrir
appear in court *v* comparecer ante el tribunal
appearance *n* comparecencia
appellant *n* apelante, recurrente
appellee *n* apelado
application *n* solicitud, petición
argue *v* argumentar, argüir, disputar
argument *n* argumento, exposición
arrears *n* atrasos, pagos en mora
article *n* artículo
assign *v* ceder, transferir
assignee *n* cesionario, apoderado
assignment *n* cesión
assignor *n* cedente
assist *v* asistir, ayudar
at your own risk *adv* bajo su cuenta y riesgo
attendance *n* asistencia
attorney *n* abogado, letrado, licenciado
attorney of record *n* abogado del caso
attorney's fees *n* honorarios profesionales
authentic *adj* auténtico, genuino, fidedigno
bad faith *n* mala fe
bailiff *n* alguacil
bar *n* colegio de abogados, obstáculo, barrera
bearer *n* portador
bench trial *n* juicio ante un juez
binding *adj* vinculante
bodily/body search *n* registro corporal
bodily injury/harm *n* daños físicos, lesiones

bond *n* bono
brain contusion *n* contusión cerebral
brain damage *n* lesión cerebral
breach *n* incumplimiento; *v* incumplir
breach of duty *n* incumplimiento del deber
brief *n* sumario, resumen
burden of proof *n* carga de la prueba
bylaws *n* estatutos, reglamento interno
cannabis *n* canabis, marihuana
case *n* caso, causa, proceso
case file *n* expediente del caso, expediente de la causa
case law *n* jurisprudencia, precedentes judiciales
caseflow management *n* administración de casos
caseworker *n* asistente social
certified mail *n* correo registrado
challenge *n* desafío; *v* desafiar, impugnar
charge to the jury *n* instrucciones al jurado
chattel *n* bien mueble
circumstantial evidence *n* prueba circunstancial
circumvent *v* circunvenir, rodear, evitar
claim *n* reclamación, reclamo, demanda; *v* reclamar,
    demandar, exigir
claimant *n* reclamante, demandante
class action *n* acción judicial colectiva, recurso de
    clase, juicio colectivo
Class Action Fairness Act (CAFA) *n* Ley de Equidad
    de Recursos de Clase
clause *n* cláusula
clinical examination *n* examen clínico
closing argument *n* alegatos finales
coca *n* coca

cocaine *n* cocaína
collect evidence *v* reunir pruebas, recabar pruebas
collection agency *n* agencia de cobranza
commission *n* comisión
commit *(confine)* *v* internar
compensatory damages *n* indemnización compensatoria
competent to stand trial *adj* capaz de someterse
    a juicio
competent to testify *adj* apto para dar testimonio
complainant *n* demandante
complaint *(civil)* *n* demanda, querella, denuncia
comply with *v* acatar, obedecer, ceñirse a
conceal *v* ocultar, esconder
conciliation *n* conciliación
condemnation *n* expropiación
confidential *adj* confidencial
consent *n* consentimiento; *v* consentir
conservatee *n* pupilo
conservator *n* curador
conservatorship *n* curatela
consolidation of actions *n* consolidación de acciones
constitution *n* constitución
constitutional *adj* constitucional, conforme a la
    constitución
consul *n* cónsul
consulate *n* consulado
consumer *n* consumidor
contempt of court *n* desacato, contumacia, rebeldía
continuance *(postponement of a trial or hearing)* *n*
    aplazamiento *(de un juicio o una audiencia)*
contract *n* contrato

contractual *adj* contractual
convention *n* convención
cop *(slang)* *n* policía, polizonte
corroborate *v* corroborar
corroborated *adj* corroborado, confirmado
corrupt *adj* corrupto; *v* corromper
corruption *n* corrupción
cosigner *n* cofirmante
cost *n* costo; *v* costar
counsel, counselor *n* asesor legal, letrado, licenciado
counterclaim *n* contrademanda; *v* contrademandar
course of conduct *n* línea de conducta
court *n* tribunal, juzgado
court clerk *n* secretario del tribunal
court clerk's office *n* secretariado del tribunal
court costs *n* costas judiciales
court of appeals *n* tribunal de apelaciones, tribunal de
    segunda instancia
court reporter *n* estenógrafo, taquígrafo judicial
courtroom *n* sala de audiencia
credibility *n* credibilidad
credible *adj* creíble
crime *n* crimen, delito
cross-claim *n* reclamo recíproco, demanda en contra
    de la co-parte
cross-examination *n* repregunta, contrainterrogatorio
cross-examine *v* repreguntar, contrainterrogar
culpability *n* culpabilidad
custody *n* custodia
custody of evidence *n* custodia de la prueba
customs *n* aduanas

damages *n* indemnización de daños y perjuicios

date *n* fecha, cita; *v* salir juntos

dead man's statute *n* regla procesal que impide alegar lo dicho por una persona difunta

death certificate *n* certificado de defunción

decedent *n* difunto, fallecido

deceive *v* engañar

declarant *n* declarante

declaration *n* declaración

declare *v* declarar

decree *n* auto, decreto; *v* decretar

deed *(action)* *n* acto, actuación

deed *(instrument transferring ownership of real property)* *n* instrumento que transfiere la propiedad de un inmueble

defamation *n* difamación

default judgment *n* fallo por incumplimiento

defend *v* defender

defendant *n* acusado, defendido, demandado

defense *n* defensa

delay *n* retraso, demora; *v* retrasar, demorar

deliberate *adj* deliberado; *v* deliberar

delinquency *n* delincuencia

delinquent *adj/n* delincuente

denial *n* rechazo

deny *v* rechazar

deny a motion *v* denegar un pedimento

deponent *n* deponente

depose *v* deponer

deposition *n* deposición, declaración jurada

direct examination *n* examen directo, interrogatorio directo

direct income withholding *n* retención directa de ingresos

disbursement *n* desembolso

disclose *v* revelar, divulgar

disclosure *n* divulgación

discontinuance *n* desistimiento

discovery *n* conjunto de medios procesales mediante los cuales las partes obtienen información sobre un litigio

dismiss *v* desestimar, sobreseir

dismissal *n* desestimación, sobreseimiento

dismissal with prejudice *n* desestimación con pérdida de derecho

dismissal without prejudice *n* desestimación sin pérdida de derecho

disposable income *n* ingreso disponible

dispute *n* querella, litigio

disqualification *n* recusación

disqualified *adj* descalificado, inhabilitado, impedido

disqualify *v* descalificar, inhabilitar

distinguish between right and wrong *v* distinguir entre el bien y el mal

district *n* distrito, partido, demarcación

district attorney *n* fiscal de distrito

district court *n* tribunal de distrito

DNA test *n* examen de ADN

docket *n* libro judicial, calendario de casos, lista de casos

documentary evidence *n* prueba documental

domicile *n* domicilio

drug *n* droga; *v* drogar

drunk *adj/n* ebrio, borracho

drunkard *n* borracho

drunkenness *n* ebriedad, borrachería

due process *n* proceso debido, garantías procesales

duty of care *n* deber de diligencia, deber de cautela

eavesdropping *n* escucha subrepticia, ilegal de
    conversaciones

eligibility *n* aptitud, capacidad, idoneidad

eligible *adj* apto, capaz, idóneo, elegible

embassy *n* embajada

eminent domain *n* poder estatal de expropriar para
    fines públicos

enforcement of judgment *n* ejecución de sentencia

enjoyment of rights *n* goce de derechos

equality under the law *n* igualdad de acuerdo con la ley

evidence *n* pruebas

evidence ruling *n* fallo probatorio

evidentiary *adj* probatorio, evidencial

examination of witness *n* examen del testigo

examine *v* examinar, interrogar

examine the facts *v* considerar los hechos, analizar
    los hechos

excited utterance *n* expresión espontánea

execute *v* ejecutar

execution *n* ejecución

executor *n* albacea testamentario

exhaustion of remedies *n* agotamiento de recursos

exhibit *n* prueba real

expert *n* perito, experto

expert examination *n* examen de perito
expert opinion *n* informe pericial, dictamen pericial
expert witness *n* perito, consultor técinco
expertise *n* pericia
expiration *n* vencimiento, caducidad
expire *v* vencer, expirar
extension *n* prórroga
extension of period of stay *n* prórroga de suspensión
extenuating *adj* atenuante
facial *adj* textual
facially *adv* textualmente
facilitate *v* facilitar
fact finding *n* investigación de hechos, determinación
    de hechos
Federal Emergency Management Agency (FEMA)
    n Agencia Federal de Gestión de Emergencias
fiduciary *adj/n* fiduciario
finding *n* determinación
fine *n* multa; *v* multar
foreman of jury *n* vocero del jurado
forensic *adj* forense
foreseeable *adj* previsible
forfeit *v* perder un derecho como consecuencia de un
    incumplimiento
fundamental right *n* derecho fundamental
gang *n* mara, banda
garnishment *n* retención de ingresos
give notice *v* notificar, dar aviso
grace period *n* período de gracia
grant a motion *v* dar lugar a un pedimento
grievance *n* queja, agravio

gross negligence *n* negligencia grave

ground *n* fundamento, base, motivo

grounds for re-trial *n* motivo para ordenar un juicio nuevo

handwriting *n* letra, escritura manuscrita

harassment *n* acoso

hardship *n* privación, adversidad

harm *n* daño, perjuicio

harmful *adj* dañino

hashish *n* hashish

hearing *n* vista, audiencia

hearsay *n* prueba de oída

heir *n* heredero

illegal *adj* ilegal, ilícito

illegal entry *n* ingreso ilegal

immigrant *n* inmigrante

immigration *n* inmigración

imminent danger *n* peligro inminente

impeach *v* impugnar

implicated *adj* involucrado

incident report *n* informe sobre los sucesos

incite *v* incitar, instigar

income *n* ingreso

induce *v* inducir, alientar

informed consent *n* consentimiento válido, información y consentimiento

inherit *v* heredar

inheritance *n* herencia, patrimonio

injunction *n* orden judicial

injured party *n* persona dañada, persona perjudicada

injury *n* daño, lesión

inquest *n* indagatoria
inquest jury *n* jurado indagatorio
inquire *v* averiguar, investigar
inquiry *n* investigación
insane *adj* demente, loco
insanity *n* demencia, locura, incapacidad mental
intend *v* tener la intención de
intention *n* propósito, ánimo
international judicial assistance *n* asistencia judicial
    internacional
interpret *v* interpretar
interpretation *n* interpretación
interpreter *n* intérprete
interrogate *v* interrogar
intestate *adj* intestado
intimidate *v* intimidar
intoxication *n* intoxicación
investigate *v* investigar, averiguar
investigation *n* investigación, pesquisa
irrebuttable presumption *n* presunción absoluta
issue *v* expedir, emitir
judge *n* juez; *v* juzgar
judgment *n* sentencia, fallo
judicial review *n* revisión, potestad revisora
jurisdiction *n* competencia, jurisdicción
jurisdictional limit *n* límite jurisdiccional
juror *n* jurado, miembro del jurado
jury *n* jurado
jury challenge *n* impugnación del jurado, recusación
    del jurado
jury charge *n* instrucciones al jurado

justice court *n* juzgado
juvenile *adj/n* menor de edad
knowingly *adv* a sabiendas
lack of jurisdiction *n* falta de jurisdicción, falta de
    competencia
law *n* ley
lawful *adj* lícito
lawsuit *n* querella
lawyer *n* abogado
leading question *n* pregunta capciosa
leave to appeal *n* permiso de apelar, autorización
    de apelar
legal *adj* legal, lícito
legal representative *n* representante legal
legalization *n* legalización
lewd conduct *n* conducta lasciva, conducta indecente
liability *n* responsabilidad legal
liable *adj* responsable
Limited English Proficiency (LEP) *adj* con
    conocimientos limitados del inglés
liquidated damages *n* daños liquidos y determinados
    *(indemnización por daños y perjuicios prefijada
    en contrato)*
litigant *n* litigante
litigate *v* litigar
litigation *n* litigio, controversia judicial, pleito
litigation cost *n* costas judiciales
magistrate judge *n* juez magistrado, juez auxiliar
malfeasance *n* fechoría
mandatory *adj* obligatorio
manslaughter *n* homicidio culposo

marijuana *n* marihuana, canabis
mediate *v* mediar
mediation *n* mediación
mediator *n* mediador
medical report *n* informe médico
mental deficiency *n* defecto mental, deficiencia mental
mental depression *n* depresión mental
mental disorder *n* desorden mental, trastorno mental,
    enfermedad mental
methamphetamine *n* metanfetamina
minor *adj/n* menor de edad
misconduct *n* mala conducta, conducta ilegal
mistake *n* error, equivocación
mistrial *n* juicio nulo
mitigating *adj* atenuante
mob *n* pandilla, banda
modify *v* alterar, modificar
motion *n* pedimento, petición
motive *n* móvil, motivo
narcotics *n* narcóticos, estupefacientes
nationality *n* nacionalidad
neglect *n* descuido; *v* descuidar
negligence *n* negligencia
negligent *adj* negligente
negligently *adv* negligentemente, descuidadamente
net worth *n* patrimonio, haber patrimonial
new trial of a case *n* nueva vista de la causa
notarial *adj* notarial
notary *n* fedatario
notify *v* notificar, dar aviso
null and void *adj* nulo e írrito

nursing home *n* hogar de ancianos

oath *n* juramento

obey *v* obedecer

objection *n* objeción

obscenity *n* obscenidad

offense *n* delito, infracción, acto ilícito

opening statement *n* exposición de apertura, alegato de apertura

operation of law (by) *adv* por ministerio de ley, de acuerdo a la ley

oral argument *n* presentación oral de argumentos

oral proceedings *n* procedimiento oral

order *n* orden; *v* ordenar

ordinance *n* ordenanza, ley municipal

overrule an objection *v* rechazar una objeción, denegar una objeción

panel of judges *n* panel de jueces

party *n* parte

passport *n* pasaporte

penalty *n* penalidad, pena, sanción

pendente lite *adj/adv* durante el juicio

period *n* período, plazo

permit *n* permiso

person *n* persona

personal jurisdiction *n* jurisdicción sobre la persona

personalty *n* bienes muebles

petition *n* solicitud; *v* solicitar

physical evidence *n* pruebas físicas, prueba real

plaintiff *n* demandante

pleading *n* alegato

police *n* policía

policeman, police officer *n* policía

postpone *v* postergar, diferir

power of attorney *n* poder, mandato

prejudicial *adj* perjudicial

preside over *v* presidir

presiding judge *n* juez que preside, juez presidente

presume *v* suponer

presumption *n* presunción

pretrial conference *n* conferencia preliminar

prima facie *adj* prima facie, a primera vista

pro se *adv* por derecho propio, actuando por su propio
derecho y sin estar representado por un abogado

probate *n* procedimiento de legalización de
testamentos

probative value *n* valor probatorio

procedure *n* procedimiento, diligencia, trámite

proceed *v* proceder

proceeding *n* procedimiento

proof *n* prueba

property *n* propiedad

proprietary *adj* propio, relativo a un derecho de
propiedad

protective order *n* orden de protección

prove *v* probar

psychiatric evaluation *n* evaluación psiquiátrica

public prosecutor *n* fiscal

puncture wound *n* punción, herida de puñalada

punitive damages *n* daños punitivos

put on notice *v* notificar oficialmente, prevenir
oficialmente, advertir oficialmente

qualified immunity *n* inmunidad limitada

quash *v* invalidar

question *v* examinar, interrogar; *n* pregunta

reasonable basis/ground *n* base razonable, motivo
   razonable

rebuttable *adj* refutable, rebatible

rebuttal *n* refutación

record of investigation *n* informe indagatorio,
   informe de investigación

re-cross examination *n* segunda repregunta

recusal *n* recusación

recuse *v* recusar

rehabilitate *v* rehabilitar

rehabilitation *n* rehabilitación

remand *v* reenviar un caso a un tribunal, devolver
   un caso a un tribunal; ordenar que un acusado
   comparezca otra vez ante determinado tribunal

removal to federal court *n* transferencia de un caso a
   nivel federal

repeal *n* anulación, revocación; *v* anular, revocar

represent *v* representar

representative *n* representante

res judicata *n* cosa juzgada

rescind *v* rescindir, resolver

rescission *n* rescisión

respondent *n* demandado

respondent on appeal *n* apelado

responsibility *n* responsabilidad

responsible *adj* responsable

resume *v* reanudar

re-trial *n* nuevo juicio

reverse *v* revocar, anular

revocation *n* revocación

revoke *v* revocar

ruling *n* fallo, dictamen

schizophrenia *n* esquizofrenia

search *n* registro, búsqueda; *v* registrar, revisar, buscar

self dealing *n* acto de interés propio por un representante, acto de interés propio por un fideicomisario

sequester *(jury)* *v* aislar *(al jurado)*

serve or deliver *(process)* *v* notificar *(actos procesales)*

service *(of process)* *n* notificación *(de actos procesales),* diligenciamiento

session *n* sesión

session (to be in ~) *v* estar en audiencia, celebrar sesión

settlement *n* transacción, arreglo

severance of proceedings *n* separación de acciones procesales

sexual intercourse *n* acceso carnal, coito

sign *v* firmar

signature *n* firma

special master *n* comisionado especial

spokesman *n* vocero

stab wound *n* punción, herida de puñalada

stalk *v* acechar

stalking *n* acto de acechar

statement *n* declaración

statute *n* ley escrita, legislación

statute of limitations *n* ley que fija términos de prescripción

statutory *adj* relativo a las leyes escritas

subject-matter jurisdiction *n* competencia en razón de la materia

suborn *v* sobornar

subornation *n* soborno

substantial error *n* error substancial

sue *v* entablar querella, intentar querella

suit *n* querella

summary *n* resumen, extracto

summary judgment *n* fallo sumario

summary proceeding *n* procedimiento sumario, procedimiento expeditivo

summation *n* sumario

summon *v* llamar, citar a comparecer

summons *n* citación, orden de comparecencia

surprise *n* sorpresa; *v* sorprender

surrender *n* entrega; *v* entregar, entregarse, rendirse

surrogate court *n* tribunal con competencia en juicios sucesorios

swear *v* jurar, prestar juramento, juramentar

tamper with *v* modificar fraudulentamente, alterar fraudulentamente

tangible *adj* tangible, corporal

term *n* término, plazo

territorial jurisdiction *n* jurisdicción territorial

testify *v* dar declarar, atestiguar

testimony *n* testimonio

threat *n* amenaza

threaten *v* amenazar

tort *n* acto ilícito civil, delito civil

tortfeasor *n* persona que comete un acto ilícito civil

tortious *adj* relativo a actos ilícitos civiles
transcript *n* transcripcón, acta taquigráfica
traumatic *adj* traumático
treaty *n* tratado
trial *n* juicio, proceso, audiencia
trial court *n* tribunal de primera instancia
trial date *n* fecha de juicio
trial procedure *n* procedimiento del juicio,
    tramitación del juicio
trial record *n* actas del juicio
truancy *n* ausentismo escolar
trust *n* fideicomiso
trustee *n* fideicomisario
unconstitutional *n* inconstitucional, contrario a la
    constitución
unless otherwise agreed *adv* salvo acuerdo contrario
user *n* usuario
usher *n* conserje
valid *adj* válido
value *n* valor; *v* valorar
verbatim record *n* acta literal
verdict *n* veredicto
visa *n* visa
voluntarily *adv* voluntariamente, a sabiendas
waive a right *v* renunciar a un derecho
waiver *n* renunciación, excepción
weapon *n* arma
will *n* testamento
willingly *adv* voluntariamente, a sabiendas
with prejudice *adj/adv* con perjuicio
withdraw *v* retirar, revocar

without prejudice *adj/adv* sin perjuicio, sin pérdida
de derecho
witness *n* testigo; *v* presenciar, observar
work-related injury *n* lesión laboral
wound *n* herida, lesión
written answer/reply *n* respuesta escrita
written statement *n* declaración por escrito
wrongful death *n* muerte por negligencia

COMMERCIAL LAW
DERECHO COMERCIAL

Commercial law deals with **contractual** and business relationships, **finance**, **banking**, **investments**, **insurance**, and rules governing the **sale** of **goods** and **services** to **consumers**.

401(k) Plan *n* Plan 401(k)
accelerated depreciation *n* depreciación acelerada
acceptance *n* aceptación
account *n* cuenta
account verification *n* verificación de cuentas
accountant *n* contador, contable
accounting *n* contabilidad
accounts payable *n* cuentas pagaderas
accrual basis (on an ~) *adv* con base en lo devengado
accrue *v* acumular, devengar
accrued interest *n* intereses acumulados, intereses
     devengados
ad valorem *n* según el valor
ad valorem duty *n* impuesto de aduana según el valor,
     derecho de aduana según el valor
adjusted gross income *n* ingreso bruto ajustado
adjusted itemized deductions *n* deducciones
     detalladas ajustadas
affiliate *n* filial

after-tax return *n* rédito neto de impuestos, rendimiento neto de impuestos

agency *n* agencia, mandato, representación

agent *n* agente, mandado

alternative minimum tax *n* impuesto mínimo alternativo

amended return *n* declaración de impuestos corregida, declaración de impuestos enmendada

amortization *n* amortización, depreciación de bienes

analyst report *n* informe del périto *(sobre inversiones y finanzas)*

annual fee *n* cuota anual

annual percentage rate (APR) *n* tasa porcentual anual

appreciation in value *n* incremento de valor, aumento de valor

arbitrage *n* arbitraje

arbitration *n* arbitraje

arrears *n* moras, pagos en mora

articles of association *n* escritura de sociedad, acta constitutiva

assess *v* valorar, valuar, tasar

assessment *n* tasación, valoración

assessor *n* tasador

asset *n* activo, bien, haber

assignment *n* cesión, transferencia

auction *n* subasta

audit *n* auditoría, inspección

audit opinion *n* dictamen de auditoría

automated teller machine (ATM) *n* cajero automático

average daily balance *n* saldo diario promedio

avoidance (tax ~) *n* reducción de la carga tributaria por medios legales

backup withholding *n* retención adicional de impuesto

bad debt *n* deuda incobrable

balance *n* saldo

balance sheet *n* hoja de balance, balance general

balanced budget *n* presupuesto equilibrado

balloon payment *n* pago global *(al vencimiento de un préstamo, el pago por la cantidad total que representa el capital adeudado)*

bank *n* banco

bank account *n* cuenta bancaria

bank check *n* cheque de cajero

Bank Secrecy Act (BSA) *n* Ley Sobre el Secreto Bancario

bank statement *n* estado de cuenta, extracto de cuenta

banking *n* la banca

bankrupt *adj* fallido, insolvente, quebrado, en quiebra

bankruptcy *n* quiebra, bancarrota, insolvencia, cesación de pagos

Bankruptcy Code *n* Código de Insolvencia

bankruptcy court *n* tribunal de insolvencia, tribunal de quiebra

bargain *n* ganga

bearer *n* portador

bearer check *n* cheque al portador

beneficial owner *n* titular beneficiario

beneficiary *n* beneficiario

benefit *n* beneficio, prestación; *v* beneficiar

benefits manager *n* gerente de beneficios

bid *n* oferta, propuesta, licitación

big board *n* la Bolsa de Nueva York

bill *n* cuenta, factura; *v* facturar

bill of exchange *n* letra de cambio

billing cycle *n* ciclo de facturación

billing error *n* error de facturación

billing inquiry *n* averiguación de facturación

billing rights *n* derechos de facturación de crédito

black market *n* mercado negro

blue laws *n* leyes estatales que en EEUU limitan las
        horas de comercio los domingos

bona fide *adj* de buena fe

bond *n* bono

bonus *n* prima, premio

book value *n* valor contable

borrow *v* pedir prestado, solicitar préstamo

borrower *n* prestatario

bounce a check *(slang)* *v* rechazarse un cheque por
        falta de fondos

breach of contract *n* incumplimiento de contrato

breach of warranty *n* incumplimiento de garantía

bridge loan *n* préstamo puente

broke *(slang) adj (estar)* bruja, sin dinero

broker *n* agente, corredor

budget *n* presupuesto

business *n* negocio

business contract *n* contrato de negocios

business days *n* días hábiles, días laborales

business expenses *n* gastos empresarios

business hours *n* horas laborales

business license *n* licencia comercial, permiso comercial

business registration *n* matrícula de comercio
businessman, *n* negociante, hombre de negocios
businesswoman *n* mujer de negocios
buyer *n* comprador
buy-sell agreement *n* acuerdo de compraventa,
      contrato de compraventa
calendar quarter *n* trimestre calendario, trimestre civil
calendar year *n* año calendario, año civil
call option *(option enabling holder to buy a security
      at a fixed price by a set date in future)* *n*
      opción de compra *(de un valor a precio fijo en
      determinada fecha futura)*
cancel *v* anular
cancellation clause *n* cláusula resolutiva
cancellation of debt *n* anulación de deuda
cancelled check *n* cheque cancelado
capital *n* capital
capital assets *n* activos fijos, activos permanentes
capital expenditure *n* gastos de capital
capital gain *n* ganancia de capital
capital gains tax *n* impuesto sobre las ganancias
      de capital
capital loss *n* pérdida de capital
capitalize *v* capitalizar
capitalized interest *n* interés capitalizado
cargo *n* carga, flete, cargamento
carry over *(a balance)* *v* traspasar *(un saldo anterior)*
cash *adj* en efectivo; *n* efectivo, numerario, contante;
      v cobrar, realizar
cash advance *n* adelanto en efectivo, anticipo en
      efectivo

Commercial Law

cash cow *(business or venture serving mainly to produce a cash flow)* *n* comercio o empresa que sirve para producir un flujo de fondos líquidos

cash crunch *n* falta de liquidez

cash flow *n* flujo de liquidez

cash machine *n* cajero automático

cashier's check *n* cheque de caja, cheque bancario, cheque de cajero

Caveat emptor. *(Let the buyer beware.)* Que tenga cuidado el comprador.

central bank *n* banco central

certificate *n* certificado

certificate of deposit (CD) *n* certificado de depósito (CD)

certified check *n* cheque certificado

certified public accountant (CPA) *n* contador público

chapter 11 bankruptcy *n* insolvencia bajo el Capítulo 11 de la Ley de Quiebras

chapter 7 bankruptcy *n* insolvencia bajo el Capítulo 7 de la Ley de Quiebras, reorganización

charge *n* cobro; *v* cobrar

charitable contribution deduction *n* deducción por donación caritativa

chartered financial consultant (ChFC) *n* consultor financiero colegiado

check *n* cheque

checking account *n* cuenta de cheques, cuenta corriente

child and dependent care credit *n* crédito por costos de cuidado de niños y dependientes

client *n* cliente, usuario

collateral *n* colateral, resguardo

collect *adj* por cobrar; *v* cobrar
collection agency *n* agencia de cobranza
commerce *n* comercio
commercial bank *n* banco comercial
commercial dispute *n* diferendo comercial
commercial law *n* derecho comercial
commercial litigation *n* litigio comercial
commission *n* comisión
commodity *n* producto básico
commodity exchange *n* bolsa de productos básicos
common stock *n* acciones ordinarias
commuting expense *n* gastos de viaje al trabajo
company *n* compañía, sociedad
company law *n* derecho de sociedades
company report *n* informe de sociedad
compensation *n* compensación, retribución
competition *n* concurrencia, competencia
competitor *n* concurrente
compliance *n* cumplimiento
compound interest *n* interés compuesto
concession *n* concesión
consideration *n* contraprestación
consignee *n* consignatario, destinatario
consignment *n* carga, envío
consolidated financial statement *n* estado contable
consolidado
consumer *n* consumidor
consumer credit *n* crédito al consumidor
Consumer Credit Counseling Service (CCCS) *n*
Servicio de Asesoría en Materia Crediticia al
Consumidor

consumer debts *n* deudas del consumidor

consumer goods *n* bienes de consumo

Consumer Protection Act *n* Ley de Protección al Consumidor

consumer reporting company *n* compañía de informes de consumidores

consumer rights *n* derechos del consumidor

contract *n* contrato, convenio, acuerdo

contract law *n* derecho de contratos

contract of guarantee *n* contrato de garantía

contract of indemnity *n* contrato de indemnidad, contrato de indemnización

contract of sale *n* contrato de venta

contracting party *n* parte contratante

contractor *n* contratante, contratista

convertible *adj* convertible

corner the market *v* acaparar, monopolizar

corporation *n* corporación, sociedad anónima

cosigner *n* cosignatario, cofirmante

counterclaim *n* contrademanda, reconvención

counteroffer *n* contraoferta

courier *n* mensajero

credit *n* crédito

credit bureau *n* agencia de reporte y clasificación de crédito

credit card *n* tarjeta de crédito

credit card agreement *n* contrato de tarjeta de crédito

credit counselor *n* consejero de crédito

credit history *n* historial de crédito

credit insurance *n* seguro sobre el crédito

credit limit *n* límite de crédito

credit line *n* línea de crédito

credit profile *n* categoría de crédito, historial de crédito

credit rating/score *n* calificación de crédito

credit rating agency *n* agencia de calificación de crédito

credit report *n* informe de crédito

credit reporting agency *n* agencia de calificación de crédito

credit union *n* cooperativa de crédito

creditor *n* acreedor

current account *n* cuenta corriente

customer *n* cliente

customer service *n* servicio al cliente

daily balance *n* saldo diario

daily periodic rate *n* tasa periódica diaria

day care center *n* guardería

dealer *n* agente, corredor, negociante

debenture *n* obligación

debit *n* débito, saldo deudor

debit card *n* tarjeta de débito

debt *n* deuda, obligación

debtor *n* deudor

deceptive *adj* engañoso

deduction *n* deducción

default *n* incumplimiento; *v* faltar, dejar de cumplir

defraud *v* defraudar, estafar

delayed *adj* demorado

delinquency *n* morosidad

delinquent *adj* en mora

dependent *adj/n* dependiente
deposit *n* depósito
depositary receipt *n* certificado de depósitos en custodia
depreciable property *n* bienes depreciables
depreciation *n* depreciación, amortización,
     desvalorización
derivatives *n* derivados
discharge *n* liberación, extinción
discharge in bankruptcy *n* extinción de deuda por
     bancarrota
discharge of contract *n* extinción de contrato
discharge of debt *n* extinción de deuda
disclosure *n* divulgación
discount *n* descuento
discount rate *n* tasa de descuento
discounted *adj* con descuento
distressed price *n* precio de liquidación
distributor *n* distribuidor
distributorship *n* sociedad distribuidora
diversify *v* diversificar
dividend *n* dividendo
dot-com company *n* compañía punto.com
double billing *n* doble facturación
double counting *n* doble contabilidad
double dipping *n* doble utilización
down payment *n* enganche, pago inicial
draft *n* letra de cambio
draw funds *v* retirar fondos
drawee *n* girado
drawer *n* girador

dual-status taxpayer *(foreign-national taxpayer who in any year changes his or her resident status from nonresident to resident alien or from resident to nonresident alien)* *n* contribuyente extranjero que durante el mismo año ha sido residente y no-residente

due date *n* fecha de vencimiento

due diligence *n* medidas cautelares, estudio realizado por el comprador para confirmar que el objeto de su interés se corresponde con el objeto esperado

dwelling *n* vivienda

early *adj* temprano, anticipado

early withdrawal penalty *n* penalidad por retiro anticipado

earned income *n* ingreso salarial, ingreso devengado a cambio de trabajo

earned income credit (EIC) *n* crédito de ingresos personales

e-banking *n* banca electrónica

e-commerce *n* comercio electrónico

e-filing *(of income tax)* *n* declaración electrónica *(de impuestos)*

electronic funds transfer (EFT) *n* transferencia electrónica de fondos

e-mail *n* correo electrónico

employee stock plan *n* plan de adquisición de acciones para empleados

employment tax *n* impuestos sobre la nómina de empleados

endorse *v* endosar

endorsement *n* endoso

Commercial Law

enterprise *n* empresa, proyecto, iniciativa

Equal Credit Opportunity Act (ECOA) *n* Ley de Igualdad de Oportunidades de Crédito

estate tax *n* impuesto sucesorio

estimated tax *n* impuesto estimado

evasion *n* evasión

exchange rate *n* tasa de cambio

excise tax *n* impuesto de consumo, impuesto indirecto

exempt assets *n* bienes exentos

exercise price *(price set in an option contract)* *n* precio de ejercicio *(de un contrato de opciones)*

expense account *n* cuenta de gastos

Fair Credit Billing Act (FCBA) *n* Ley de la Justa Facturación

Fair Credit Reporting Act (FCRA) *n* Ley de Emisión de Informes Crediticios Equitativos

Fair Debt Collection Practices Act *n* Ley de Cobranza Imparcial de Deudas

fair market value (FMV) *n* valor justo de mercado

false advertising *n* publicidad fraudulenta

fax, facsimile *n* fax, facsímile

Federal Deposit Insurance Corporation (FDIC) *n* Corporación Federal de Seguro de Depósitos

Federal Reserve Bank (FRB) *n* Banco Federal de Reserva

Federal Trade Commission (FTC) *n* Comisión Federal de Comercio

fee *n* honorario, cuota

fiduciary *n* fiduciario

file *n* archivo; *v* archivar, presentar, entablar

filing status *n* estado civil para la declaración de impuestos

finance *n* finanza; *v* financiar

finance charge *n* costo financiero, costo de financiamiento

financial advisor *n* consejero financiero

financial investigator *(IRS agent)* *n* investigador financiero, investigador fiscal

financial statements *n* estados financieros

financial transaction *n* operación financiera

first mortgage *n* hipoteca de primer rango

fiscal year *n* año fiscal

flat rate *n* tarifa fija, tasa fija

flexible spending account (FSA) *n* cuenta de gastos flexible

float *(loans, bonds, etc.)* *v* emitir *(préstamos, bonos, etc.)*

foreign earned income *n* ingresos devengados en el extranjero

form *n* formulario

Form W-2 *n* Formulario W-2

Form W-4 *n* Formulario W-4

Fortune 500 *n* la lista "Fortune 500" de las principales empresas

franchise *n* concesión comercial

franchisee *n* franquiciado, concesionario, agente autorizado

franchisor *n* franquiciador

fraudulent conveyance *n* transferencia fraudulenta de bienes

freeze *(assets, deposits, etc.)* *v* congelar *(activos, depósitos, etc.)*

freight *n* flete

fringe benefit *n* beneficio marginal, prestación marginal

fund *n* fondo

funding *n* financiación

funds *n* fondos

General Anti-Avoidance Rule (GAAR) *n* Norma General de Antievasión Impositiva

General Fraud Program *n* Programa General contra el Fraude Impositivo

gift tax *n* impuesto sobre donaciones

golden parachute *n* acuerdo que otorga indemnización superior a los ejecutivos en caso de que cambie su situación en la compañía como resultado de una acquisición por parte de otro grupo

good faith *n* buena fe

gratuity *n* propina

grieve *v* entablar queja

gross *adj* en bruto

gross dividends *n* dividendos brutos

gross income *n* ingreso bruto, renta bruta

gross sales *n* ventas brutas

half-year report *n* informe semestral

hardship *n* privación, apuro económico, situación económica difícil

head of household *n* jefe de familia

heading of document *n* encabezamiento de documento

hedge *v* protegerse contra riesgos o pérdidas

hedge fund *n* fondo de cobertura, fondo de alto riesgo

high-risk investment *n* inversión de alto riesgo

historic financial statements *n* estados financieros
    históricos
home equity loan *n* préstamo garantizado por el valor
    liquido de su hogar
home office *n* oficina a domicilio
home-based business *n* negocio en casa
homeowner *n* dueño de casa
homeworker *n* empleado casero, persona que trabaja
    desde su casa
HOPE scholarship credit *n* crédito tributario para
    estudiantes inscritos al menos medio tiempo
    en uno de los dos primeros años de educación
    universitaria
hostile takeover *n* toma de control hostil
in kind *adj/adv* en especie *(no en dinero)*
income tax *n* impuesto sobre la renta
incoming *adj* entrante
incorporate *(a company)* *v* constituir legalmente *(una
    sociedad)*
incur *v* incurrir, acumular
indemnification *n* indemnización
indemnify *v* indemnizar, compensar
independent contractor *n* contratista independiente
individual retirement account (IRA) *n* cuenta de
    retiro individual
initial public offering (IPO) *n* oferta pública inicial
insider trading *n* operaciones en base a información
    confidencial
insolvency *n* insolvencia
insolvent *adj* insolvente
installment *n* pago parcial, cuota

Commercial Law

instrument *n* instrumento, documento
insurance *n* seguro
insurance premium *n* prima de seguro
insured *adj* asegurado
interest *n* interés
interest expenses *n* gastos por concepto de intereses
interest income *n* ingreso por concepto de intereses
interest rate *n* tasa de interés
Internal Revenue Code (IRC) *n* Código de Impuestos, Código Tributario
Internal Revenue Service (IRS) *n* Servicio de Impuestos Internos
inventory *n* inventario, existencias
invest *v* invertir
investment *n* inversión
investment account *n* cuenta de inversiones
investment committee *n* comité de inversiones
investment company *n* sociedad de inversiones
investment counselor *n* consejero, asesor de inversiones
investment strategy *n* estrategia de inversiones
investment vehicle *n* instrumento de inversión, entidad instrumental para inversiones
investor *n* inversionista, inversor
invoice *n* factura, cuenta
IOU *n* pagaré
itemized deductions *n* deducciones detalladas
joint account *n* cuenta conjunta
joint return *n* declaración de impuestos conjunta
kickback *n* comisión confidencial
know your client (KYC) *n* conozca a su cliente

late charge *n* cobro por tardanza, cobro por demora
late filing penalty *n* multa por declaración retrasada
late payment *n* pago retrasado
layoff *n* despido temporal
lease *n* arrendamiento
ledger *n* libro mayor
legal tender *n* moneda corriente
lend *v* prestar
lender *n* prestador, prestamista
letter of credit *n* carta de crédito
letterhead *n* membrete
liability *n* responsabilidad legal
liability insurance *n* seguro de responsabilidad legal
license *n* licencia
lien *n* gravamen, derecho de retención
lien holder *n* titular de gravamen
life insurance *n* seguro de vida
Lifetime Learning Credit *n* Crédito tributario de
    Aprendizaje de por Vida
limited liability *n* responsabilidad limitada
liquid asset *n* activo líquido
liquidation *n* liquidación
liquidity *n* liquidez
listed company *n* sociedad cotizante, que cotiza en la
    bolsa de valores
loan *n* préstamo
loan consolidation *n* préstamo que combina y refinancia
    otros créditos o deudas
loan officer *n* responsable de préstamos
local taxes *n* impuestos locales

London Interbank Offered Rate (LIBOR) *n* tasa
    LIBOR
loss *n* pérdida
lump-sum payment *n* pago global
luxury goods *n* artículos de lujo
mail *n* correo
mailbox *n* buzón
management *n* gestión
manager *n* gerente
manufacturer *n* fabricante
market *n* mercado
market rate *n* tasa de mercado
market value *n* valor de mercado
marketing *n* mercadotécnica
married filing jointly/separately *adj* declaración
    de impuestos *(por personas casadas)* de forma
    conjunta/separada
matter *n* asunto
maturity *n* vencimiento
Medicare tax *n* impuesto Medicare
meeting of the minds *n* acuerdo entre partes
    contratantes
merchandise *n* mercancía
merchant *n* negociante, comerciante
merchant bank *n* banco de inversión
merchantable *adj* comerciable, vendible
merger *(of companies)* *n* fusión *(de sociedades)*
mergers and acquisitions *n* fusiones y adquisiciones
minimum payment *n* pago mínimo
monetary compensation *n* compensación monetaria
money laundering *n* lavado de dinero

money market *n* mercado monetario
money market account *n* cuenta del mercado monetario
money order *n* giro, libranza
money transfer *n* transferencia de fondos
moneylender *n* prestamista
mortgage *n* hipoteca
moving expenses *n* gastos de mudanza
municipal bond *n* bono municipal
mutual fund *n* fondo mutuo, fondo de inversión
National Taxpayer Advocate *n* Defensor Nacional
    del Contribuyente
net *adj* neto
net earnings *n* ingresos netos
net profit *n* ganancia neta, utilidad neta
net sales *n* ventas netas
net worth *n* haber patrimonial, patrimonio
night deposit *n* depósito nocturno
no-competition clause *n* cláusula de abstención de
    competencia
nominee *n* apoderado
non-compliance *n* incumplimiento
nonprofit *adj* sin fines de lucro
nonwage payments *n* pagos que no son de sueldo
note *n* pagaré
offer *n* oferta; *v* ofrecer
offeree *n* quien recibe una oferta
offering circular *n* prospecto abreviado de emisión
    de valores
offeror *n* oferente
offshore *adj* offshore, ultramar
online *adj* en línea

Commercial Law

online banking *n* servicios bancarios en línea
oral contract *n* contrato oral
ordinary dividend *n* dividendo ordinario
outstanding balance *n* saldo pendiente
overbilling *n* facturación excesiva
overdraft *n* descubierto, sobregiro
overdraft checking *n* cuenta de cheques con línea
    de credito
overdraw *v* sobregirar
overlimit charge *n* cargo por sobregiro
overpayment *n* pago en exceso
overstate *n* exagerar el valor de algo
owe *v* deber
par value *n* valor nominal
parent company *n* sociedad controlante, sociedad
    matriz, casa matriz
partner *n* socio
partnership *n* sociedad
password *n* clave personal, contraseña
pay off *v* saldar, liquidar
payable *adj* pagadero
payable at sight *adj* pagadero a la vista
paycheck *n* pago de sueldo, pago por nómina, cheque
    de nómina
payee *n* beneficiario
payment *n* pago
payor *n* pagador
payroll tax *n* cargas sociales
penalty *n* penalidad
pension *n* pensión
pension fund *n* fondo para jubilados y pensionados

personal check *n* cheque personal

personal exemptions *n* exenciones personales

personal identification number (PIN) *n* número de
    identificación personal, clave personal

pirated copyright goods *n* bienes de marca pirateados

poison pill *n* estrategia defensiva de una compañía
    para encarecer notablemente una compra hostil
    de sus acciones

preferred *adj* preferente

premature withdrawal *n* retiro anticipado

prepackaged *adj* precombinado

previous balance *n* saldo anterior

price *n* precio

price gouging *n* exageración de precios

prime rate *n* tasa de interés preferencial

principal *n* capital, principal

privacy policy *n* política de confidencialidad

private company *n* compañía privada

private letter ruling *n* declaración escrita expedida
    a un contribuyente que interpreta y aplica las
    leyes fiscales

pro forma *adj* pro forma

pro rata *adj* prorrata

proceeds *n* producto, réditos

produce *v* producir

product *n* producto

product liability *n* responsabilidad por productos
    defectuosos

production *n* producción

productivity *n* productividad

profit *n* ganancia, utilidad, lucro

Commercial Law

profit and loss account *n* cuenta de pérdidas y ganancias
profit sharing *n* reparto de ganancias
progressive tax *n* impuesto progresivo
promissory note *n* pagaré, vale
property tax *n* impuesto sobre bienes inmuebles, impuesto a la propiedad inmobiliaria
prorate *v* prorratear
prospectus *n* prospecto, folleto
proxy statement *n* carta poder
publicity *n* publicidad
publicly traded company *n* sociedad cotizante, sociedad que cotiza en bolsa
purchase *n* compra, adquisición; *v* comprar, adquirir
purchase price *n* precio de compra, precio de adquisición
put option *(option enabling holder to sell a security at a set price by a set date in future)* *n* opción de venta *(de un valor a precio fijo en determinada fecha futura)*
qualified audit opinion *n* dictamen con salvedades
qualifying widow(er) *n* viuda(o) que reúne los requisitos
quarterly *adj* trimestral
Racketeer Influenced Corrupt Organizations Act (RICO) *n* Ley de Organizaciones de Crimen Organizado y Corruptas
rate of return *n* tasa de rédito
raw material *n* materia prima
real time *adj* instantáneo
realize *v* realizar, convertir en dinero
receipt *n* recibo

receivable *n* activo exigible, efecto a cobrar
recipient *n* destinatario
recover *v* recuperar
recovery *n* obtención de sentencia favorable
refund *n* reembolso, devolución
registration *n* registro, matrícula, inscripción
reimburse *v* reembolsar
reimbursement *n* reembolso, devolución
release note *n* constancia de liberación de hipoteca
renewal of contract *n* extensión de contrato,
        renovación de contrato
rent *n* renta, alquiler; *v* rentar, alquilar
repay *v* reembolsar, reintegrar
repayment period *n* plazo de reembolso
replenish *v* reabastecer
repossess *v* recuperar *(un bien)*
rescind *v* rescindir, anular, abrogar
rescission *n* rescisión, anulación, abrogación
restructuring *n* reorganización
retail *adj* de menudeo, al detalle
retire a debt *v* cancelar una deuda
retirement plan *n* plan de jubilación
return *n* rédito, producto
return on investment (ROI) *n* rédito de inversión
reverse mortgage *n* hipoteca revertida
revolving account *n* cuenta de crédito renovable
Roth IRA *n* cuenta de retiro individual Roth
royalty *n* derecho de autor
royalty income *n* ingreso por derechos de autor
sale *n* venta

sale and purchase agreement *n* contrato de
  compraventa
sale price *n* precio de venta
sales tax *n* impuesto sobre las ventas
save *v* ahorrar
savings *n* ahorros
savings account *n* cuenta de ahorros
savings bond *n* bono de ahorro
scam *(slang)* *n* estafa
schedule *n* lista, programa, cuadro, tarifa
scholarship *n* beca
school tax *n* impuesto escolar
secured party *n* acreedor privilegiado
secured transaction *n* operación garantizada
securities *(stocks, bonds, etc.)* *n* valores, títulos
securitization *n* securitización, titularización
self-employment tax *n* impuesto sobre el ingreso de
  trabajadores independientes
sell *v* vender
sell off *v* liquidar
seller *n* vendedor
sender *n* remitente
service contract *n* contrato de servicio
setoff *n* compensación
share *n* acción
ship *v* embarcar, consignar
shipment *n* cargamento, consignación
short selling, shorting *v* venta corta, venta en descubierto
single *(filing status)* *adj* soltero *(contribuyente)*
small business *n* pequeño negocio, pequeña empresa

Small Business Administration (SBA) *n* Agencia Federal Para el Desarrollo de la Pequeña Empresa

small claims *n* controversias de cuantía menor

Social Security *n* seguro social

Social Security benefits *n* beneficios de seguridad social, prestaciones de seguridad social

Social Security income *n* ingreso de seguro social

Social Security Number (SSN) *n* número de seguro social

Social Security tax *n* impuesto de seguro social

solvent *adj* solvente

standard deductions *n* deducciones normales

state tax *n* impuesto estatal

stock *n* acciones

stock exchange *n* bolsa de valores

stock market *n* mercado de valores

stop payment *v* suspender un pago

streamline *v* agilizar

strict products liability *n* responsabilidad civil por productos defectuosos

subsidiary *n* subsidiaria

supplier *n* proveedor

supply *n* oferta, abastecimiento; *v* proveer, abastecer

surcharge *n* sobrecargo

swing loan *n* préstamo puente

take over *v* tomar posesión, hacerse cargo

takeover bid *n* oferta pública de adquisición de valores

tariff *n* arncel

tax *n* impuesto; *v* imponer impuestos, recaudar impuestos

tax assessment *n* tasación impositiva

Commercial Law

tax bracket *n* tipo impositivo, tramo fiscal

tax collector *n* recaudador de impuestos

Tax Court *n* Tribunal Tributario

tax credit *n* crédito tributario

tax deductible *adj* desgravable

tax deduction *n* gasto deducible

tax deferred *adj* sujeto a impuesto diferido

tax exempt *adj* exento de impuestos, libre de impuestos

tax exemption *n* exención de impuestos, exoneración de impuestos, franquicia de impuestos

tax law *n* derecho impositivo, derecho tributario

tax liability *n* deuda tributaria

tax preparer *n* preparador de formularios de impuestos

tax rate *n* tasa impositiva

tax refund *n* reembolso de impuestos

tax relief *n* reducción fiscal

tax return *n* declaración de impuestos

tax shelter *n* refugio fiscal

tax treaty *n* tratado fiscal, acuerdo fiscal

taxable *adj* sujeto a impuesto

taxpayer *n* contribuyente

taxpayer advocate *n* defensor del contribuyente

Taxpayer Advocate Service *n* Servicio del Defensor del Contribuyente

TeleFile *n* declaración de impuestos mediante internet

teller's check *n* cheque de caja

term life insurance *n* seguro de vida a plazo

termination of contract *n* rescisión de contrato, anulación de contrato

thrift institution *n* institución de ahorros, caja de ahorros

time deposit *n* depósito a plazo

tip *n* propina

trade *n* comercio, operación comercial

trade secret *n* secreto comercial

trader *n* negociante, comerciante, mercader

trades *n* operaciones

trading volume *n* volumen operado

traditional IRA *n* IRA tradicional

transaction *n* operación

transaction fees/costs *n* costos de negociación

transfer agent *(agent responsible for registration or retention of securities records)* *n* agente de transferencias *(de valores)*

traveler's check *n* cheque de viajero

treasury bill *n* letra del tesoro

trust fund *n* fondo fiduciario

Truth in Lending Act (TILA) *n* Ley de Veracidad en los Préstamos

turn-around *n* plazo, lapso

turnover tax *n* impuesto sobre el volumen de negocios

unauthorized withdrawal *n* retiro indebido

underpayment *n* pago insuficiente

underpayment penalty *n* penalidad por pago insuficiente

underreport *v* sub-declarar *(ingreso),* sub-registrar *(datos)*

underwriter *n* asegurador

unemployment benefits *n* beneficios de desempleo

unfair competition *n* competencia desleal

Uniform Commercial Code *n* Código Comercial Uniforme (de EE UU)

Uniform Fraudulent Transfers Act (UFTA) *n* Ley
Uniforme sobre Transferencias Fraudulentas
unlawful gains *n* ganancias ilegales
unrealized loss or profit *n* pérdida o ganancia no
realizada
upload electronic data *v* cargar datos electrónicos
use tax *n* impuesto al uso
value *n* valor
value added tax (VAT) *n* impuesto de valor añadido
vending machine *n* dispensador automático
vendor *n* vendedor
verbal contract *n* contrato verbal, contrato de palabra
voicemail *n* mensajes de voz, correo vocal
void *adj* nulo; *v* anular, cancelar
warrant *(certificate issued to holders of securities
giving them the right to buy securities at a
set price in future)* *n* warrant *(certificado que
da derecho a comprar valores a precio fijo en
el futuro)*
warranty *n* garantía
wholesale *adj* de mayoreo, al por mayor
winding up *n* conclusión, liquidación
wire transfer *n* envío de fondos por transferencia
electrónica
wireless *adj* inalámbrico, móvil
withdraw *v* retirar
withdrawal *n* retiro
withhold *v* retener
withholding tax *n* impuesto retenido, retención de
impuesto
worth *n* haber, patrimonio

write off *(debt)* *n* valor pasado a perdidas; *v* cancelar,
    anular *(deuda)*
write-off account *n* cuenta incobrable anulada
written contract *n* contrato por escrito
written notice *n* aviso por escrito

CRIMINAL LAW
DERECHO PENAL

Criminal law, also known as **penal law**, deals with acts which society treats as **punishable** offenses. According to an ancient principle, *nulla poena sine lege* ("there is no crime without a law"), acts are not punishable until a law has been passed making them so. Under provisions against **double jeopardy,** a person who has been **acquitted** (found innocent) cannot be tried again for the same crime. The **accused** facing **prosecution** generally enjoys certain safeguards in mounting his **defense** under **criminal procedure** codes, and if **convicted** (found guilty) will be punished according to the seriousness of the crime, with penalties ranging from **fines** for **misdemeanors** (minor offenses) to **sentences** of **imprisonment** or even death for **felonies** (serious offenses). In the United States, criminal matters are governed by both state and federal laws.

abduct *v* secuestrar, raptar
abduction *n* secuestro, rapto
abductor *n* secuestrador, raptor
abstract of judgment *n* resumen de fallo
acceptance of responsibility *n* aceptación de
    responsabilidad
accessory *n* partícipe
accessory after the fact *n* encubridor

Criminal Law

accomplice *n* cómplice
accuse *v* acusar
accused *adj/n* inculpado, acusado
acquit *v* absolver, exculpar
acquittal *n* absolución, fallo absolutorio
acquitted *adj* absuelto, exculpado
adjusted offense level *n* determinación penal ajustada
admission *n* admisión
adverse witness *n* testigo adverso
affidavit *n* declaración jurada por escrito
affirmative defense *n* defensa afirmativa
aggravated *adj* agraviado
aggravated felony *n* delito grave con circunstancias
     agravantes
aggravating circumstances *n* circunstancias
     agraviantes
aid and abet *v* auxiliar, colaborar, ser cómplice
alibi *n* coartada
allocution *n* alocución *(declaración hecha antes de
     la sentencia por un acusado que se ha declarado
     culpable)*
alternative sentence *n* sanción no-carcelaria
amnesty *n* amnistía
armed career criminal *n* criminal de carrera armado
arraign *v* acusar formalmente, leer los cargos
arraignment *n* instrucción de cargos, lectura de
     cargos, vista incoatoria, acto de acusación formal
arrest *n* arresto; *v* arrestar
arrest history/record *n* antecedentes penales, ficha
     policial
arrest warrant *n* orden de detención

arresting officer *n* agente/policía que efectúa el arresto

arson *n* delito de incendio

assault *n* agresión, ataque

assault and battery *n* agresión/ataque a una persona con contacto físico agresivo

assault with a deadly weapon *n* agresión con arma mortífera

attempt *n* intento, tentativa; *v* intentar

auto stripping *n* desmantelamiento de vehículos

auto tampering *n* desmantelamiento de vehículos

bail *n* fianza de descarcelación

bail bondsman *n* fiador judicial

bail hearing *n* vista de fianza

bail package *n* fianza compuesta

Bail Reform Act *n* Ley de Reforma de Fianzas

bailiff *n* alguacil

bailor *n* fiador

base offense level *n* nivel penal básico de un delito

battery *n* agresión, acto de agredir con violencia, atacar físicamente

beyond a reasonable doubt *adv* fuera de toda duda razonable

bigamist *n* bígamo

bigamy *n* bigamia

bill of particulars *n* exposición revelatoria

bind over *v* consignar, conminar

Blood Alcohol Level (BAC) *n* Concentración de Alcohol en la Sangre (CAS)

book *v* registrar, reseñar, fichar un arrestado

booking *n* reseña, ficha de arrestado

Criminal Law

breaking and entering *n* acto de entrar por la fuerza, allanamiento

bribe *n* soborno; *v* sobornar

bribery *n* soborno

brief *n* escrito, relación, memorial

bug *(slang)* *v* vigilar por medios electrónicos

burden of proof *n* carga de la prueba

burglar *n* ladrón, escalador nocturno

burglar's tools *n* instrumentos para allanamientos

burglary *n* allanamiento de morada, robo con escalo

capital offense *n* delito con pena de muerte

capital punishment *n* pena de muerte, pena capital

carrying a firearm *n* posesión de arma de fuego

cell *n* celda

challenge a decision *v* impugnar una decisión

charge *n* cargo, punto de acusación; *v* acusar, cobrar

charged *adj* imputado, acusado

circumstantial evidence *n* prueba circunstancial, prueba indirecta

civil collections *n* cobranza civil

clemency *n* clemencia, indulto

co-conspirator *n* co-conspirador

code of criminal procedure *n* código de procedimientos penales

coercion *n* cohecho, coacción

collateral for bail *n* garantía para fianza

collection of evidence *n* recolección de pruebas, recabación de pruebas, obtención de pruebas

commission of a crime *n* ejecución de un delito

commit a crime *v* cometer un delito

commitment order *n* orden de encarcelamiento**

community service *n* trabajos comunitarios

complaint *(criminal)* *n* denuncia

concurrent sentence *n* pena concurrente, pena simultánea

conditional plea of guilty *n* declaración condicional de culpabilidad

conditional release *n* libertad supervisada, libertad sujeta a condiciones

conditions of release *n* condiciones de libertad condicional

confession *n* confesión

confine *v* internar, encarcelar

confinement *n* internamiento, encarcelamiento

confiscate *v* confiscar

consecutive sentence *n* pena sucesiva, pena consecutiva

conspiracy *n* conspiración, complot, conjura, asociación delictiva

conspirator *n* conspirador, conjurador

conspire *v* conspirar, conjurar

contraband *n* contrabando

contributing to the delinquency of a minor *v* contribuir a la corrupción de un menor de edad

convict *n* reo, preso; *v* condenar, declarar culpable

convicted *adj* convicto, condenado

conviction *n* condena

cooperation agreement *n* acuerdo de cooperación

cooperation with the prosecution *n* cooperación con la fiscalía

correctional center *n* centro correccional

corrupt *adj* corrupto, doloso; *v* corromper, sobornar

corruption *n* corrupción

count of indictment *n* cargo, motivo de acusación, punto de acusación

counterfeit *adj* falso, falsificado

counterfeiter *n* falsario

counterfeiting *n* falsificación de moneda

crime *n* delito

crime of moral turpitude *n* delito de vileza moral

crime of passion *n* crimen pasional

crime of violence *n* delito de violencia, delito violento

criminal history category *n* categoría penal según los antecedentes penales

criminal negligence *n* negligencia dolosa

criminal history/record *n* antecedents penales

criminal trespass *n* entrada ilícita

culpable *adj* culpable

custody *(of a person)* *n* custodia judicial, tutela *(de una persona)*

cybercrime *n* ciberdelito

cyberstalking *n* acoso a través de internet

date rape *n* violación durante una cita

deadly force *n* fuerza mortífera

deadly weapon *n* arma mortífera

death penalty *n* pena de muerte, pena capital

defense *n* defensa

defense attorney *n* abogado defensor

defense preparation period *n* período para la preparación de la defensa

defraud *v* estafar

Department of Homeland Security *n* Departamento de Seguridad Interior

deport *v* deportar

deportable *adj* deportable, expulsable

deportation *n* deportación

deportation hearing *n* audiencia de deportación

detective *n* detective

detention *n* detención

disciplinary proceedings *n* procedimientos disciplinarios

dismissal of charges *n* sobreseimiento de los cargos

disorder *(physical or mental)* *n* trastorno *(físico o mental)*

disqualification *n* descalificación, recusación

disturbing the peace *n* alteración del orden público, alboroto

diversion program *(system permitting first offenders for lesser crimes under conditional release to perform community service, make restitution or obtain substance abuse treatment and/or counseling)* *n* programa de rehabilitación y/o servicio comunitario

double jeopardy *n* doble juzgamiento por la misma causa, riesgo de ser enjuiciada una persona en la misma jurisdicción más de una vez por el mismo delito

dragnet *n* redada

driving while intoxicated (DWI) *n* conducir un vehículo en estado de ebriedad

drug dealer *n* traficante de estupefacientes

drug trafficker *n* traficante de estupefacientes

drug trafficking offense *n* delito relacionado al tráfico de estupefacientes

duress *n* coerción, coacción

electronic monitoring *n* supervisión electrónica
electronic surveillance *n* vigilancia electrónica
embezzlement *n* desfalco, malversación
enter a plea *v* asentar una declaración
entrapment *n* trampa policíaca
escape *n* fuga; *v* fugarse
evidentiary hearing *n* vista probatoria
excessive bail *n* fianza excesiva
exculpatory evidence *n* pruebas eximentes, exculpatorias
exonerate *v* exonerar
expunge *v* expurgar
extenuating circumstances *n* circunstancias
    eximientes, circunstancias atenuantes
extortion *n* extorción, exacción
eyewitness *n* testigo ocular
face charges *v* responder a los cargos
false imprisonment *n* detención ilegal, detención
    injustificada, encarcelamiento ilegal
false pretenses *n* declaraciones fraudulentas,
    declaraciones engañosas
fear *n* miedo, temor
Federal Bureau of Prisons *n* Dirección Federal de
    Prisiones
federal offense *n* delito federal
Federal Rules of Evidence *n* Normas Probatorias
    Federales
felon *n* criminal, autor de un delito grave
felony *n* delito grave, delito mayor
felony murder *n* homicidio resultante de otro delito
    grave

Fifth Amendment right against self-incrimination
n garantía de la Quinta Enmienda contra la
autoincriminación *(garantía contenida en la
Quinta Enmienda de la Constitución de los
Estados Unidos que permite a un sospechoso o
acusado negarse a hacer cualquier declaración
que podría incriminarlo)*

fight *n* lucha, pelea, combate, riña; *v* pelear, luchar

final sentence *n* sentencia firme

fingerprints *n* huellas digitales, huellas dactilares

firearm *n* arma de fuego

first degree murder *n* asesinato agravado o premeditado

first offense *n* primera infracción

flee *v* huir

flight *n* huida, fuga

force *n* fuerza; *v* forzar

forfeit bail *v* incautarse la fianza

forfeiture *n* decomiso

forger *n* falsificador, fabricante de documentos falsos

forgery *n* falsificación de un documento o billete con
intención de defraudar

fraud *n* fraude, estafa, engaño

fraudulent *adj* fraudulento, engañoso

frisk *v* palpar, cachear

fugitive *n* fugitivo, prófugo

gambling *n* envite, juegos de azar, hacer apuestas

gang *n* pandilla, banda, mara

general intent *n* dolo, dolo directo

go to trial *v* pasar a juicio

good behavior time *n* remisión de la duración de la
pena por buen comportamiento

Criminal Law

grand jury *n* jurado indagatorio, jurado de acusación
grand larceny *n* hurto mayor
guilty *adj* culpable
gun *n* pistola
gunman *n* pistolero
habeas corpus *n* mandato de habeas corpus
habitual offender *n* reincidente
handcuffs *n* esposas
harassment *n* acoso
hate crime *n* crimen de odio, crimen motivado por odio
Hobbs Act *n* Ley Hobbs
holding cell *n* celda de detención temporal
home detention *n* detención en el hogar, detención domiciliaria
hooker *(slang for **prostitute**)* *n* ramera *(jerga por prostituta)*
hostage *n* rehén
hostage taking *n* toma de rehenes
house arrest *n* retención domiciliaria
hung jury *n* jurado en desacuerdo
identity theft *n* robo de identidad
ill-treatment *n* tratamiento vejatorio, maltrato
impossibility *n* imposibilidad
imprisonment *n* encarcelamiento
in absentia *adv* en rebeldía
inadmissible evidence *n* prueba improcedente
inadmissible to the U.S. *adj* inadmisible a los EE UU
incest *n* incesto
indecent exposure *n* exhibición obscena
independent evidence *n* prueba independiente
indeterminate sentence *n* pena indeterminada

indictment *n* documento inculpatorio, acusación formal
infancy *n* minoridad, infancia
informant *n* informante, informador
information *n* informe acusatorio
informer *n* delator
infraction *n* falta, infracción
injured party *n* el agraviado
inmate *n* recluso
innocence *n* inocencia
innocent *adj* inocente
insufficient evidence *n* pruebas insuficientes
intent *n* intención, propósito, ánimo
intentionally *adv* intencionalmente, deliberadamente,
    a propósito
intercept *n* intervención *(de comunicación privada)*;
    v interceptar
intermittent sentence *n* pena intermitente, sentencia
    intermitente
intoxication *n* intoxicación, ebriedad
investigate *v* investigar, averiguar
investigation *n* investigación
investigator *n* investigador, detective
irresistible impulse *n* impulso irresistible
jail *n* cárcel
Jencks Act *n* Ley Jencks
joinder of offenses *n* acumulación de delitos
juvenile offender *n* delincuente juvenil
kidnapping *n* secuestro, rapto, sustracción de menores
knowingly *adv* a sabiendas, deliberadamente
larceny *n* hurto, robo de poca importancia
law enforcement methods *n* métodos policíacos

Criminal Law

law enforcement official/officer *n* agente encargado de hacer cumplir la ley

leniency *n* indulgencia, lenidad

lenient *adj* indulgente, poco severo

letter: 5K letter *(letter by the prosecutor stating that the accused has provided substantial assistance to the prosecution)* *n* carta 5K *(carta del fiscal por la que se consta que el acusado ha proporcionado ayuda substancial a la fiscalía)*

life sentence *n* reclusión perpetua, cadena perpetua

light sentence *n* pena leve

lineup *n* cuerda de reos, cuerda de sospechosos, rueda de sospechosos

loan sharking *n* usura

long arm jurisdiction *n* jurisdicción entre estados

looting *n* saqueo

malice *n* malicia, mala intención, dolo, alevosía

malicious *adj* malicioso

malicious mischief *n* daños dolosos

maliciously *adv* maliciosamente

mandatory minimum sentence *n* pena mínima obligatoria

mastermind *n* autor intelectual

mayhem *n* mutilación criminal

minimal participant *n* conspirador con participación mínima

minor participant *n* conspirador con participación menor

Miranda warning *n* alerta Miranda, advertencia según el caso Miranda (see Appendix 2)

misconduct *n* mala conducta

misconduct before the Court *n* falta ante la Corte

misdemeanor *n* delito menor

misdemeanor court *n* alcaldía, tribunal de delitos menores

Model Penal Code *n* Código Penal Modelo

money laundering *n* blanqueo de dinero, lavado de dinero

morgue *n* morgue

motion after trial *n* petición después de el juicio

motion to limit the use of evidence *n* petición para limitar el uso de la prueba

motion to suppress evidence *n* petición para suprimir pruebas

mugger *n* asaltante

murder *n* asesinato

murderer *n* asesino

necessity *(defense of)* *n (defensa de)* necesidad

no contest *n* nolo contendere *(locución latina: no se opone o acepta la acusación)*

non-jail sentence *n* sanción no-carcelaria

not guilty *adj* no culpable

notary public *n* funcionario certificador

obstruction of justice *n* obstrucción de la actividad judicial

offender *n* infractor, delincuente, transgresor, malhechor

offense *n* delito

offense level *n* nivel del delito

operating a business of prostitution *v* mantener un negocio de prostitución

organized crime *n* crimen organizado, organización criminal

Criminal Law

outcry testimony *(testimony admitted as an exception to the hearsay rule concerning what was confided to an adult witness by a person, especially a minor, with knowledge of the crime)* n testimonio "de confidencias" *(testimonio admitido, a pesar de la regla general contra pruebas de oídas, sobre lo que confió al testigo adulto una persona, especialmente un menor, con conocimiento del delito)*

pandering *(for prostitution)* n proxenetismo, lenocinio

pardon n indulto

parole n libertad supervisada, libertad sujeta a condiciones

parole board n junta de libertad vigilada

parole hearing n vista de libertad vigilada

parole officer n oficial de libertad vigilada

PATRIOT Act n Ley PATRIOT

penal *adj* penal

penalty n castigo, pena, sanción

penitentiary n penitenciaria, presidio, centro penitenciario

peremptory challenge *(of juror)* n recusación perentoria, recusación preventiva, recusación sin causa *(de jurado)*

perp *(slang for **perpetrator**)* n perpetrador

perpetrator n perpetrador, autor de un delito

persistent offender n reincidente

petition n solicitud, petición, pedido; v solicitar

physical harm n daño corporal

physical restraint n coacción física

pick a pocket v robar del bolsillo

pickpocket *n* carterista

pimp *n* alcahuete, proxeneta

pimping *n* proxenetismo, lenocinio

plea agreement *n* convenio declaratorio, conformidad del imputado, preacuerdo

plea bargain *n* convenio declaratorio, conformidad del imputado, preacuerdo

plea-bargaining *n* negociación o pacto entre el fiscal y la defensa acerca de los cargos y la pena antes de que el demandado se declare culpable

plea of innocence or guilt *n* declaración de inocencia o culpabilidad

possession *n* posesión, tenencia

post bail *v* pagar la fianza

post-release supervision *n* vigilancia de persona liberada

precedent *n* precedente

prejudicial *adj* lesivo

premeditated *adj* premeditado

preponderance of the evidence *n* preponderancia de las pruebas

pre-sentence investigation report *n* informe de investigación antes de la sentencia

presumption *n* presunción, suposición

presumption of innocence *n* presunción de inocencia

pretrial detention *n* detención antes del juicio, detención preventiva

pretrial services department *n* departamento de servicios antes del juicio

pretrial statements *n* declaraciones hechas por testigos antes del juicio

prior conviction *n* condena anterior

Criminal Law

prior juvenile offense *n* delito juvenil anterior
prison *n* prisión, cárcel
prison guard *n* guardia, celador
prisoner *n* prisionero, preso, recluso
probable cause *n* causa razonable, motivo fundado
    para sospechar
probation *n* libertad condicional, libertad probatoria
probation hearing *n* vista relativa a la libertad
    condicional
probation officer *n* agente de vigilancia de libertad
    condicional
procurer *n* proxeneta
procuring *n* proxenetismo
proffer *n* oferta
profiling *n* tendencia a singularizar como sospechosas
    a las personas que pertenecen a ciertos grupos
prohibit *v* prohibir
prohibited *adj* prohibido
prosecute *v* enjuiciar
prosecuting officer *n* oficial de la fiscalía
prosecution *n* fiscalía
prosecution witness *n* testigo de cargo
prosecutor *n* fiscal
prostitute *n* prostituta
prostitution *n* prostitución
proximate cause *n* causa inmediata
public defender *n* defensor público, defensor de oficio
punitive *adj* punitivo
qualified immunity *n* inmunidad calificada
questioning of witness on direct examination *n*
    examen del testigo por el fiscal

Racketeer Influenced and Corrupt Organizations Act (RICO) *n* Ley Sobre Organizaciones Delictivas

racketeering *n* extorción sistematizada, chantaje e intimidación

ransom *n* rescate *(pago para liberar a un rehén)*

rap sheet *n* lista de antecedentes

rape *n* violación; *v* violar

reasonable basis *n* fundamento suficiente

reasonable doubt *n* duda razonable

rebut *v* rebatir, refutar

rebuttable presumption *n* presunción rebatible, presunción refutable

rebuttal *n* dúplica

receiving stolen property (act of ~) *n* acto de recibir artículos robados, ser receptor de artículos robados

recidivist *n* reincidente

reckless endangerment *n* imprudencia temeraria

recklessly *adv* temerariamente

recklessness *n* imprudencia temeraria

record of convictions *n* antecedentes penales

record of questioning *n* levantamiento de acta de interrogatorio

record on appeal *n* expediente de apelación

recusal *n* recusación

reformatory *n* reformatorio, establecimiento penitenciario para jóvenes

release on bail *n* libertad bajo fianza; *v* liberar bajo fianza

released *adj* liberado

relevant conduct *n* conducta pertinente

Criminal Law

remanding order *n* orden de remisión
remove *(an alien from the country)* *v* trasladar,
    expulsar *(a un extranjero del país)*
renunciation *n* renunciación
reparation *n* reparación, indemnización
repeat offender *n* reincidente
re-sentencing *n* nueva sentencia
respondent on appeal *n* el apelado
restitution *n* indemnización, restitución
reversal *n* revocación, anulación
review *(immigration)* *n* petición de revisión *(de
    categoría migratoria)*
right to trial *n* garantía de audiencia
robbery *n* hurto
Rosario rule *(rule requiring complete disclosure of
    all pretrial statements of prosecution witnesses)*
    n regla según el caso Rosario *(regla que requiere
    que se revelen completamente todas las
    declaraciones hechas por los testigos de cargo
    antes del juicio)*
Rules of Criminal Procedure *n* Reglamento de
    Procedimiento Penal
safety valve *n* válvula de escape
sanction *n* sanción, castigo; *v* sancionar, castigar
sealed indictment *n* acusación formal secreta por el
    Gran Jurado
search *n* allanamiento, cateo, revisión, registro;
    v allanar, revisar
search and seizure *n* registro e incautación
search warrant *n* orden de allanamiento, orden de
    revisión

security classification *n* clasificación por razones de
    seguridad en una penitenciaria

seize *v* tomar, incautar, confiscar, aprehender

seizure *n* toma, incautación, confiscación, decomiso,
    embargo, aprehensión

self-defense *n* auto-defensa, defensa propia

self-incrimination *n* autoinculpación

self-surrender *n* acto de rendirse por cuenta propia,
    acudir uno mismo a la carcel para cumplir su pena

sentence *n* sentencia, pena; *v* sentenciar, imponer pena

sentence above/below the guideline range *n* pena
    mayor/menor a la prevista en las pautas

sentencing guidelines *n* pautas de sentencia

sentencing hearing *n* vista de sentencia

serious bodily injury *n* lesiones graves

serve a sentence *v* purgar sentencia, cumplir sentencia

settling of accounts *n* ajuste de cuentas

severance of proceedings *n* separación de autos

sexual abuse *n* abuso sexual

sexual predator *n* agresor sexual, depredador sexual

sheriff *n* alguacil, sheriff

shoot *v* tirar, disparar

shoot to kill *v* tirar a matar

shoplifter *n* ladrón ratero, mechero de tiendas

shoplifting *n* hurto en tiendas, ratería en tiendas

smuggle *v* contrabandear, hacer contrabanda, pasar de
    contrabando

smuggler *n* contrabandista, traficante

smuggling *n* contrabando

solicitation *(for prostitution)* *n* proxenetismo, lenocinio

specialized skill *n* destreza especial, habilidad especial

Criminal Law

specific intent *n* intención específica
Speedy Trial Act *n* Ley de Juicio sin Demora
stab *v* apuñalar
state *n* estado
state of mind *n* ánimo, estado mental
statement *n* declaración, afirmación, comunicado
status *n* estado, condición, categoría
statute *n* ley *(promulgada por la legislatura)*
statute of limitations *n* ley de plazo de prescripción,
     ley de expiración
statutory rape *n* estupro, relaciones sexuales con
     un menor
stay enforcement of the judgment *v* suspender la
     ejecución de la sentencia
stickup *(slang for **robbery**)* *n* atraco
strict liability *n* responsabilidad objetiva
subpoena *n* comparendo, citación, orden de
     comparecencia; *v* citar, emplazar a comparecer
substantial assistance to the government *n* ayuda
     substancial a la fiscalía
sufficient reason to suspect *n* causa razonable,
     motivo fundado para sospechar
summons *n* emplazamiento, orden de comparecencia
supervening cause *n* causa superveniente
suppression hearing *n* vista sobre la exclusión de
     pruebas
suppression of evidence *n* exclusión de pruebas
surrender *v* entregar, rendirse
surveillance *n* vigilancia
surveillance tape *n* grabación de investigación
suspect *n* sospechoso; *v* sospechar

swear *v* jurar

sworn *adj* jurado, juramentado, bajo juramento

tamper with *v* alterar, falsificar

tampering with jury *n* acto de sobornar o influir sobre el jurado

tax evasion *n* fraude tributario

Temporary Protection Status (TPS) *n* Estado de Protección Temporal

terrorism *n* terrorismo

terrorist *n* terrorista

theft *n* robo

three strikes statute *n* ley de tres chanzas

ticket (traffic ~) *n* boleta por infracción de tránsito

time in prison *n* período de encarcelamiento

time off for good behavior *n* tiempo que se descuenta de la pena por buen comportamiento

time served *n* período de encarcelamiento ya cumplido

tip off *v* pasar el dato, avisar, informar

traffic infraction *n* boleta por infracción de tránsito

traffic ticket *n* boleta por infracción de tránsito

transfer of proceedings *n* remisión del proceso

truancy *n* ausentismo escolar

try *v* enjuiciar, procesar

uncorroborated *adj* no corroborado, no confirmado

undercover operation *n* operativo encubierto

undercover police officer *n* agente policíaco encubierto, agente policíaco infiltrado

underworld *n* hampa

undocumented *n* indocumentado, sin papeles, sin documentación

Criminal Law

**United States Citizenship and Immigration
   Services (USCIS)** *n* Oficina de Ciudadanía y
   Servicios de Inmigración de los Estados Unidos
United States Code *n* Código de los Estados Unidos
United States Sentencing Commission *n* Comisión
   Federal de Sentencias
unpunished *adj* impune
usury *n* usura
vandalism *n* vandalismo
vehicular manslaughter *n* homicidio culposo por el
   conductor de un vehículo
victim *n* víctima
victim impact statement *n* declaración de los efectos
   del delito sobre la víctima o su familia
voluntary manslaughter *n* homicidio cometido
   voluntariamente pero en circunstancias de
   emoción violenta o por capacidad mental
   disminuida
voluntary surrender *n* rendición voluntaria, entrega
   voluntaria
vulnerable victim *n* víctima vulnerable
warden *(of a prison)* *n* director de una penitenciaria
warrant *n* orden, mandamiento
warrantless search *n* revisión sin mandamiento
weapon *n* arma
willful *adj* intencional, voluntario, deliberado
willfully *adv* voluntariamente
wire *(slang: recording device usually worn under
   clothing by an undercover agent)* *n* dispositivo
   oculto para grabar conversaciones
wiretap *v* interceptar líneas telefónicas

wiretap recording *n* grabación de vigilancia de líneas
    telefónicas
withdraw from a conspiracy *v* retirarse de una
    conspiración
without bail *adv* sin derecho a fianza
witness protection plan *n* plan de protección de testigos

FAMILY LAW
DERECHO DE FAMILIA

Family law deals with family events and relationships such as **birth** and **marriage,** or its dissolution (**separation** or **divorce**), laying down rules to ensure **support** for **dependents** and protecting the interests of **children.** A **judgment** of divorce may contain provisions on **custody** and **visitation** regulating the divorced parents' duties and rights with respect to minor children. Laws may also exist defining requirements for marriage, such as reaching a **marriageable age,** or setting conditions under which a marriage may be **annulled** or under which a **pre-nuptial agreement** between spouses may be enforced.

abandonment of marital domicile *n* abandono del
   domicilio conyugal
abortion *n* aborto
absolute divorce *n* divorcio en firme
actual separation *n* separación real
administrator of estate *n* administrador de
   patrimonio
adolescent *n* adolescente
adopt *v* adoptar
adoption *n* adopción
adoption tax credit *n* crédito tributario de adopción

Family Law

adoptive *adj* adoptivo
adulterer *n* adúltero
adultery *n* adulterio
Aid to Families with Dependent Children (AFDC)
   n Ayuda a Familias con Niños en Condición de
   Dependiente
alimony *n* pensión alimentaria
annulment of marriage *n* anulación de matrimonio
artificial insemination *n* inseminación artificial,
   fecundación artificial
assignment of support rights *n* asignación de
   derechos de manutención
aunt *n* tía
battered *adj* golpeado *(m)*, golpeada *(f)*
battered child *n* niño golpeado *(m)*, niña golpeada *(f)*
battered spouse *n* cónyuge golpeada(o)
beneficiary *n* beneficiario
best interests of the child *n* bienestar del menor
bigamist *n* bígamo
bigamy *n* bigamía
biological parent *n* padre natural, padre biológico
birth *n* nacimiento
birth certificate *n* certificado de nacimiento, acta de
   nacimiento
birth control *n* contracepción
born (to be ~) *v* nacer
brother *n* hermano
brother-in-law *n* cuñado
child *n* niño
child care center *n* guardería

Derecho de Familia

child support *n* pensión alimenticia, sostenimiento de un menor, mantenimiento de un menor, manutención

child support enforcement agency/office *n* agencia/oficina de cumplimiento de la manutención de los hijos

child support guidelines *n* pautas sobre mantenimiento de menores

childbirth *n* parto, alumbramiento

common law marriage *n* matrimonio resultante del consentimiento y cohabitación de las partes

community property *n* propiedad en común

competency *(of persons)* *n* capacidad *(de personas)*

competency hearing *n* vista sobre capacidad

condom *n* condón, preservativo

condonation *n* condonación

consanguinity *n* consanguinidad

consent *n* consentimiento; *v* consentir

constructive abandonment *n* abandono implícito

contraception *n* anticoncepción

contraceptive *n* anticonceptivo

counseling *n* consejos, terapia

couple *n* pareja

cousin *n* primo

cruelty *n* crueldad

custodial abduction *n* retención de un menor por una persona que no goza de custodia legal

custodial parent *n* padre con custodia, padre con tutela

custody *n* custodia

daughter *n* hija

daughter-in-law *n* nuera

deadbeat dad *(slang) n* padre que no cumple su deber de mantenimiento

death certificate *n* acta de defunción

deceased *adj* muerto, difunto, fallecido

decedent *n* difunto, fallecido

Department of Social Services *n* Departamento de Servicios Sociales

dependent *adj/n* dependiente

dissolution of marriage *n* disolución matrimonial

distributee *n* beneficiario de una herencia

divided custody *n* división de custodia

divorce *n* divorcio; *v* divorciar

divorce decree *n* acta de divorcio

divorced *adj* divorciado

divorcee *n* divorciado(a)

DNA *n* ADN

domestic *adj* doméstico

domestic partner *n* socio doméstico

domestic relations *n* relaciones familiares

domestic violence *n* violencia doméstica, violencia familiar

duty to support *n* obligación de mantener

earnings assignment *n* asignación de ingresos

earnings withholding order *n* orden de retención de ingresos

emancipate *v* emancipar

emancipated minor *n* menor emancipado, menor responsable de sí mismo

engagement to marry *n* esponsales

estate *n* patrimonio del difunto

estate tax *n* impuesto sucesorio

executor *n* albacea
ex-husband *n* ex-esposo
ex-wife *n* ex-esposa
faithful *adj* fiel
false pretenses *n* declaraciones fraudulentas, engaño
family *n* familia
family court *n* tribunal de familia, juzgado de familia
family court judge *n* juez de lo familiar
family law *n* ley de familia
family planning *n* planificación familiar
family reunification *n* reunificación familiar
father *n* padre
father-in-law *n* suegro
Federal Case Registry of Child Support *n* Registro
 Federal de Causas referidas a la Manutención de
 los Hijos
Federal Parent Locator Service *n* Servicio Federal
 de Ubicación de Padres
fertile *adj* fecundo
fiancé *n* novio
fiancée *n* novia
fidelity *n* fidelidad
final decree of divorce *n* acta definitiva de divorcio
foreign marriage *n* matrimonio contraído en el
 extranjero
foster care *n* cuidado de crianza, acogida provisional
foster parent *n* padre o madre de acogida
garnishment *n* retención
gay marriage *n* matrimonio gay, matrimonio homosexual
gift tax *n* impuesto sobre donaciones
grandchild *n* nieto *(m)*, nieta *(f)*

Family Law

granddaughter *n* nieta
grandfather *n* abuelo
grandmother *n* abuela
grandparents *n* abuelos
grandson *n* nieto
grounds for divorce *n* causales de divorcio
guardian *n* curador
guardian ad litem (GAL) *n* curador ad litem, tutor
    ad litem
guardianship *n* tutela
guidance *n* consejos
guidance counselor *n* consejero
guidelines *n* pautas
head of household *n* jefe de familia
home *n* hogar
homosexual *adj/n* homosexual
husband *n* marido
illegitimate *adj* ilegítimo
impediment to marriage *n* impedimento para casarse
impotence *n* impotencia
impotent *adj* impotente
in vitro fertilization *n* fecundación in vitro
incapacitated *adj* incapacitado
income withholding *n* retención de ingresos
incompetent person *n* persona incapaz
infertile *adj* infértil
infertility *n* infertilidad
infidelity *n* infidelidad
injunction against molestation *n* orden judicial que
    ordena a una persona abstenerse de molestar a un
    cónyuge separado

in-laws *n* parientes políticos
intestate *adj* sin testamento
irreconcilable differences *n* desavenencias
joint custody *n* custodia conjunta
juvenile *adj* juvenil, menor; *n* menor
kinship *n* parentesco
legal custody *n* custodia legal
legal separation *n* separación legal
legitimate *adj* legítimo
lesbian *n* lesbiana
living separate and apart *n* viviendo aparte y separados
lover *n* amante
maintenance *n* sostenimiento, cuota alimentaria, manuntención
marital asset *n* bien matrimonial
marital property *n* propiedad matrimonial
marital settlement agreement *n* acuerdo de resolución matrimonial
marriage *n* casamiento, matrimonio
marriage ceremony *n* ceremonia matrimonial, boda
marriage certificate *n* acta de matrimonio
marriage counseling *n* consejo matrimonial, asesoramiento matrimonial
marriage counselor *n* consejero matrimonial
marriageable age *n* edad de contraer matrimonio
married *adj* casado
marry *v* casarse
maternity leave *n* licencia por maternidad
maternity ward *n* clínica de maternidad
matrimonial *adj* matrimonial

matrimony *n* matrimonio
medical certificate *n* certificado médico
midwife *n* partera
minor *(child)* *adj/n* menor de edad
miscarriage *n* aborto espontáneo
mother *n* madre
motherhood *n* maternidad
mother-in-law *n* suegra
neglect of child *n* descuido de niño, negligencia de
    niño, abandono de niño
nephew *n* sobrino
niece *n* sobrina
no-fault divorce *n* divorcio sin falta, divorcio
    administrativo
nursery *n* guardería
offspring *n* descendencia, progenie
orphan *n* huérfano; *v* dejar huérfano
paramour *n* amante
parent(s) *n* padre(s)
parental *adj* paternal, maternal
parental rights *n* derechos paternales, derechos
    maternales
parenting class *n* curso para formación de padres
paternity *n* paternidad
paternity proceeding *n* juicio de paternidad
paternity suit *n* juicio de paternidad
physical custody *n* custodia física
pregnancy *n* embarazo
pregnant *adj* embarazada, encinta
premature birth *n* nacimiento prematuro
pre-nuptial agreement *n* acuerdo prematrimonial

probate *n* procedimiento sucesorio, legalización de testamentos

puberty *n* pubertad

putative father *n* padre putativo

putative spouse *n* cónyuge putativo

recognize *(child)* *v* reconocer *(hijo)*

reconciliation *n* reconciliación

relief *n* ayuda, remedio

remarry *v* contraer nuevas nupcias

retirement *n* jubilación

right of election by surviving spouse *n* derecho del cónyuge sobreviviente de recibir parte del patrimonio del cónyuge fallecido

Safe Child and Families Act *n* Ley de Protección del Niño y la Familia

same-sex marriage *n* unión entre miembros del mismo sexo

separate property *n* propiedad separada, propiedad individual

separated *adj* separado

separation agreement *n* acuerdo de separación

settlement *n* transacción, arreglo, composición

shared custody *n* custodia compartida

sibling *n* hermano *(m)*, hermana *(f)*

single *adj* soltero

sister *n* hermana

sister-in-law *n* cuñada

sole custody *n* custodia exclusiva, custodia única

solemnize *(marriage)* *v* solemnizar, celebrar, formalizar *(matrimonio)*

son *n* hijo

Family Law

son-in-law *n* yerno

split custody *n* separación de la patria potestad, custodia separada

spousal abuse *n* abuso del cónyuge, maltrato del cónyuge, violencia conyugal

spousal support *n* mantenimiento del cónyuge

spouse *n* cónyuge

stepfather *n* padrastro

stepmother *n* madrastra

sterility *n* infecundidad

stillborn *adj* nacido muerto

support *n* mantenimiento, sostenimiento

surrogate court proceeding *n* juicio sucesorio

surrogate mother *n* madre portadora

teenage *adj* adolescente

teenager *n* adolescente

temporary aid for needy families *n* ayuda temporal para familias necesitadas

temporary custody *n* custodia temporal, custodia provisional

temporary order *n* orden temporal

temporary restraining order (TRO) *n* orden provisional de cesar cierta conducta, resolución judicial provisonal

twins *n* gemelos, mellizos

uncle *n* tío

uncontested divorce *n* divorcio administrativo, divorcio voluntario

underage *adj* menor de edad

unfaithful *adj* infiel

use and possession of marital domicile *n (derecho de)* usar el domicilio conyugal

visitation *(of children by separated parent)* *n* visita *(de hijos por padre separado)*

visitation rights *(of children by separated parent)* *n* derechos de visita *(de los hijos por padre separado)*

wage withholding *n* retención de sueldo

waiting period *(for divorce)* *n* período de espera *(antes de declararse el divorcio)*

well-being *n* bienestar

wet-nurse *n* nodriza

widow *n* viuda

widower *n* viudo

wife *n* esposa

HEALTH-CARE LAW
DERECHO DE SALUD

Health-care law deals with **injuries, diseases,** and other medical conditions that require medical **treatment,** how **insurance** coverage is obtained and provided for such treatment under public and private plans, and how the **practice** of **medicine** and the sale of **medicines** are regulated to protect the public against risks to health and **malpractice.**

access *n* acceso
accident *n* accidente
accidental death and dismemberment *n* muerte accidental y desmembramiento
acute *adj* agudo
acute care *n* cuidado intensivo
addiction *n* adicción
additional coverage *n* cobertura adicional
adequate care *n* cuidado adecuado
adult day services *n* servicios diarios para adultos
allowance *n* asignación
ambulatory *adj* ambulatorio
appeal process *n* procedimiento de apelación
appendicitis *n* apendicitis
appointment *n* cita
asbestos *n* asbesto
assisted living *n* vivienda asistida

at-home nursing care *n* atención de enfermería en casa
bandage *n* venda
behavioral health *n* salud del comportamiento, salud
    conductal
beneficiary *n* beneficiario
beneficiary designation *n* designación de beneficiario
benefit *n* beneficio
blindness *n* ceguera
cancer *n* cáncer
cancer care *n* atención médica contra el cáncer
capitation *n* presupuesto operacional de un plan de
    seguro de salud
carcinogen *n* carcinógeno
cardiac care *n* atención cardiológica
care *n* atención
caregiver *n* cuidador
cavity *n* carie
childhood disease *n* enfermedad de la infancia
chronic *adj* crónico
chronic disease *n* enfermedad crónica
claim *n* reclamación; *v* reclamar
clinic *n* clínica
collect unemployment compensation *v* recibir
    beneficios por desempleo
common carrier coverage *n* seguro de recorrido,
    seguro de transporte
compensation *n* compensación
compensation system *n* sistema de compensación
comprehensive coverage *n* cobertura integral
consent to treatment *v* consentir al tratamiento
contact lenses *n* lentes de contacto

controlled substance *n* substancia controlada

co-payment *n* co-pago

coverage *n* cobertura

covered benefit *n* servicio amperado, beneficio
    cubierto, servicio cubierto

cure *n* remedio, cura; *v* curar

cut *n* cortada

deaf *adj* sordo

deductible *adj* deducible

denial *n* rechazo

dental *adj* dental

dentist *n* dentista

deny *v* denegar, rechazar

deny necessary treatment *v* denegar tratamiento
    necesario

dependable *adj* confiable

diabetes *n* diabetes

disability *n* discapacidad

disability benefit *n* prestación bajo seguro de
    dependencia o discapacidad

disabled *adj* discapacitado

disease *n* enfermedad

disease prevention *n* prevención de enfermedades

doctor *n* doctor, médico

domestic violence *n* violencia doméstica

drug *n* droga

drug-resistant *adj* resistente a las drogas

easy access to *n* acceso fácil a

elder *n* anciano, persona mayor

elder care *n* cuidado de ancianos, cuidado de
    envejecientes

elder law *n* derecho de ancianos, derecho de
    envejecientes
elderly *adj* anciano, mayor
eligible *adj* elegible, apto
emergency room *n* sala de emergencias, sala de
    urgencias
entitled to benefits *adj* con derecho a prestaciones
excluded risk *n* riesgo excluido
exclusion *(policy)* *n* exclusión *(de la póliza)*
expertise *n* pericia, conocimientos especializados
exposure and disappearance coverage *n* cobertura
    contra muerte accidental
eyeglasses *n* lentes, anteojos
Family Health Law *n* Ley de Salud Familiar
fertility services *n* servicios de fertilidad
first-aid kit *n* botiquín de primeros auxilios
fitness *n* aptitud física, forma física
fracture *n* fractura
free *adj* gratuito
free access *n* acceso gratuito
general practitioner *n* médico general, médico
    de familia
geriatrics *n* geriatría
grievance *n* queja, reclamación
handicap *n* incapacidad, invalidez, desventaja
handicapped *adj* incapacitado
healer *n* curandero
health *n* salud
health care *n* atención médica
health-care management *n* gestión sanitaria
health-care proxy *n* poder de atención médica

health maintenance organization (HMO) *n*
    organización para el mantenimiento de la salud
healthy *adj* saludable
home attendant *n* auxiliar de casa
hospital *n* hospital
hospitalized *adj* hospitalizado
ill *adj* enfermo, indispuesto
illness *n* enfermedad, mal, afección, dolencia
impotence *n* impotencia
incapacity *n* incapacidad
infection *n* infección
infectious disease *n* enfermedad contagiosa
informed consent *n* consentimiento informado
injury *n* lesión
insurance *n* seguro
insurance carrier *n* compañía de seguro
insurance policy *n* póliza de seguro
insured *adj* asegurado
insurer *n* compañía de seguro
intensive care *n* cuidados intensivos
lead paint *n* pintura a base de plomo
legal access *n* acceso legal
legally blind *adj* ciego según la pauta legal
legally incapacitated *adj* legalmente incapacitado
life-threatening *adj* amenaza de muerte
living will *n* directiva anticipada
loss *n* pérdida
loss of both hands and feet *n* pérdida de ambas
    manos y ambos pies
loss of entire sight *n* pérdida total de la vista
loss of hearing *n* pérdida de audición

loss of life *n* pérdida de vida
loss of speech *n* pérdida del habla
loss of thumb and index finger of the same hand *n*
    pérdida del pulgar y del índice de la misma mano
malpractice *n* mala praxis, negligencia profesional
malpractice claim *n* reclamo por negligencia
    profesional
managed care *n* atención integrada
Medicaid *n* Medicaid *(atención médica a individuos y*
    familias de recursos escasos)
medical *adj* médico
medically necessary treatment *n* tratamiento médico
    necesario
Medicare *n* Medicare
medicine *n* medicina
meet *v* satisfacer, cumplir con
mental *adj* mental
mental handicap *n* incapacidad mental
mental health *n* salud mental
mental retardation *n* retraso mental
minimum standards *n* pautas mínimas
mute *adj* mudo
neglect *n* descuido, negligencia
non-traditional medicine *n* medicina no tradicional
notice of claim *n* aviso de reclamo
nurse *n* enfermera *(f)*, enfermero *(m)*
nursing care *n* atención de enfermería, servicio de
    enfermera
nursing home *n* hogar de ancianos, hospicio para
    ancianos
nutrition *n* nutrición

obesity *n* obesidad
occupational health *n* salud laboral, higiene laboral
operating room *n* sala de operaciones, quirófano
optometrist *n* optometrista
out-patient *n* paciente externo, paciente no
    hospitalizado; *adj.* externo, no hospitalizado
over-the-counter drugs *n* medicinas sin receta médica
overweight *adj* con exceso de peso
pain *n* dolor
payment of claim *n* pago de solicitud, pago de reclamo
pending claim *n* solicitud pendiente, reclamo pendiente
permanent disability *n* invalidez permanente
permanent total disability *n* invalidez total permanente
permanent total disability benefit *n* beneficio
    relativo a la invalidez total permanente
physical handicap *n* incapacidad física
physical injury *n* lesión corporal
physical therapy *n* terapia física
physician *n* médico
pill *n* píldora
plan *n* plan
plan allowance *n* asignación, cuota según el plan
policy *n* póliza
policy benefit *n* prestación de acuerdo a la póliza
policy limit *n* límite de la póliza
policyholder *n* asegurado, tenedor, titular de una
    póliza de seguro
practitioner *n* profesional
premium *(insurance)* *n* prima *(de seguro)*
prenatal health *n* salud prenatal
prescription *n* receta médica, prescripción

prescription drug coverage *n* cobertura para
    medicamentos por receta médica
prescription drugs *n* medicamentos con receta médica
prevent *v* prevenir, evitar
prevention *n* prevención
preventive *adj* preventivo
preventive medicine *n* medicina preventiva
preventive screening *n* examen preventivo
preventive services *n* cuidado preventivo
private insurance *n* seguro privado
professional *adj* profesional
proof of loss *n* prueba de la pérdida
provider *n* proveedor
provider-patient relationship *n* relación proveedor-
    paciente
psychiatrist *n* psiquiatra
psychiatry *n* psiquiatría
quality of life *n* calidad de vida
recovery room *n* sala de recuperación
referral *n* referencia
referral line *n* línea de referencia
referral service *n* servicio de referencia
rehabilitation *n* rehabilitación
root canal therapy *n* terapia de conducto radicular,
    tratamiento de conducto
senior citizen *n* persona mayor
senior services *n* servicios para personas mayores
sexually transmitted disease *n* enfermedad
    sexualmente transmisible
sick *adj* enfermo
standards *n* pautas, normas

subscriber *n* subscriptor, abondado
substandard care *n* atención inadecuada
surgeon *n* cirujano
surgery *n* cirugía
survivor *n* sobreviviente
temporary disability *n* incapacidad temporal
terminate *v* terminar, finalizar, concluir
test *n* prueba; *v* probar
therapy *n* terapia
tonsilitis *n* amigdalitis
tonsils *n* tonsilas, amigdalas
toxic *adj* tóxico
traditional medicine *n* medicina tradicional
treat *v* tratar
treatment *n* tratamiento
unemployment *n* desempleo
utilization review *n* revisión de utilizacion
waive *v* renunciar a
weight *n* peso
weight loss *n* pérdida de peso
weight management *n* control de peso
welfare *n* bienestar, servicios sociales
will *n* testamento
workman's compensation *n* compensación laboral,
    compensación del trabajador
written notice of claim *n* reclamo escrito, reclamo
    por escrito

HOUSING LAW
DERECHO DE VIVIENDA

Housing law deals with the rules that govern **real property**, how **housing** units such as apartments must be used and **maintained**, **rental agreements**, **leases**, **mortgages**, and the rights and duties of **landlords** and tenants. In the United States, state and local laws govern most housing-law issues.

abandon *v* abandonar
abandonment of premises *n* abandono del local
acceleration clause *n* cláusula de caducidad de plazos
access to premises *n* acceso al local
accessory *adj* accesorio
accessory apartment *n* apartamento accesorio
accessory use *n* uso accesorio
adjustable rate mortgage (ARM) *n* préstamo o
    hipoteca de tasa ajustable
administrator's deed *n* escritura de propiedad
    adquirida mediante administración sucesoria
adverse possession *n* prescripción adquisitiva
appraisal *n* valuación, avalúo, tasación
assessed value *n* valor de tasación
assignment of lease *n* cesión de arrendamiento
balloon mortgage *n* hipoteca de pago global
    acelerado

bargain and sale deed *n* título mediante compraventa, escritura mediante compraventa

base rent *n* renta básica

blockbusting *n* acoso inmobiliario (hacer entender implícita o explícitamente que la composición racial o religiosa de una área o vecindario va a cambiar, y que éste cambio resultará en consecuencias desastrosas, con el propósito de inducir transacciones inmobiliarias)

builder *n* constructor, sociedad constructora

building *n* edificio, inmueble

buydown *n* descuento de hipoteca mediante pago de puntos extra

cession deed *n* título por cesión, escritura por cesión

closing *n* finalización, cierre

closing costs *n* costes de finalización

commercial lease *n* arrendamiento comercial

common elements *n* elementos comunes

constructive eviction *n* desalojo presunto

convey *v* transferir *(bienes raíces)*

conveyance *n* acto de transmisión de propiedad, título de transmisión de propiedad

cost approach *n* método de valuación según costos

court-ordered eviction *n* desalojo por orden judicial

covenant *n* convenio contractual, estipulación contractual

covenant against encumbrances *n* garantía de que un inmueble se encuentra libre de grávamenes

covenant of quiet enjoyment *n* garantía de que el adquirente no se verá afectado por acciones o derechos de terceros

deed *n* instrumento/escritura mediante el que se transfieren derechos sobre un inmueble, título de propiedad

deed of correction *n* escritura correctiva

deed of gift *n* instrumento de donación

deed of trust *n* escritura de fideicomiso

defeasible fee *n* derecho de dominio condicional, derecho de dominio contingente, derecho de dominio revocable, derecho de dominio imperfecto

deposit *n* depósito

direct costs *n* costos directos

easement *n* servidumbre

equity *n* capital invertido en un inmueble

estate *n* propiedad, patrimonio, derecho relativo a inmuebles

estate at sufferance *n* posesión legítima de un inmueble en virtud de la tolerancia del propietario

estate at will *n* derecho a la posesión de un inmueble que puede darse por terminado en cualquier momento por quien lo concedió

estate for years *n* derecho relativo a inmuebles de duración fija

evict *v* desalojar

eviction *n* desalojo

executor's deed *n* instrumento (o escritura) de propiedad adquirido mediante un albacea

expiration of lease term *n* vencimiento de arrendamiento

fair housing *n* vivienda justa

**Federal Home Loan Mortgage Corporation
    (Freddie Mac)** *n* Corporación Federal de
    Hipotecas de Préstamos para la Vivienda
Federal Housing Administration (FHA) *n*
    Administración Federal de Vivienda *(Agencia
    federal, parte de HUD, que garantiza préstamos
    hipotecarios para proteger a los acreedores; no
    otorga préstamos hipotecarios, pero protege a los
    acreedores contra pérdidas)*
fee simple *n* derecho pleno de dominio sobre inmuebles
fee simple absolute *n* derecho pleno de dominio sobre
    inmuebles no sujeto a limitaciones o condiciones
fence *n* cerca, valla
fixture *n* instalación
foreclose *v* ejecutar una hipoteca
foreclosure *n* ejecución hipotecaria
full covenant and warranty deed *n* escritura de
    propiedad con garantías plenas
graduated lease *n* locación de alquiler variable según
    las ventas del locatario u otro parámetro
grant *n* concesión
grantee *n* donatario
grantor *n* donante
ground lease *n* locación de un terreno
habitable *adj* habitable
heating *n* calefacción
holding period *n* período de tenencia
holdover tenant *n* locatario u otro tenedor (inquilino)
    que retiene un inmueble una vez expirados sus
    derechos

home equity line of credit *n* línea de crédito sobre el valor acumulado de la propiedad

home equity loan *n* préstamo hipotecario sobre el valor de la propiedad

house *n* casa

housing *n* vivienda, alojamiento

housing court *n* tribunal de vivienda

housing project *n* urbanización, proyecto de vivienda

insured value *n* valor asegurado

involuntary lien *n* derecho de preferencia o privilegio independiente del consentimiento del obligado

joint tenancy *n* copropiedad sobre un inmueble de tal manera que al fallecer un copropietario sus derechos pasan a los restantes, con duración común y similares derechos posesorios

judicial deed *n* escritura (o título) mediante acto judicial

junior mortgage *n* hipoteca subordinada

landlord *n* propietario, arrendador

lease *n* arrendamiento; *v* arrendar

lease agreement *n* contrato de arrendamiento

lease expiration *n* vencimiento del arrendamiento

lease term *n* plazo de arrendamiento

lease-hold estate *n* propiedad en arrendamiento

lessee *n* arrendatario

lessor *n* arrendador

lien *n* gravamen *(privilegio o derecho de preferencia de un acreedor)*

life estate *n* propiedad vitalicia

lis pendens *(Latin) n* litispendencia

littoral rights *n* derechos de propietario ribereño

loan-to-value ratio *n* razón de préstamo a valor

lot *n* lote, solar, parcela

low-income housing *n* vivienda para personas de ingresos limitados

maintain *v* mantener

maintenance *n* mantenimiento

market value *n* valor de mercado

materialman's lien *n* gravamen a favor de un proveedor de materiales

mechanic's lien *n* gravamen del constructor

metes and bounds *n* límites o linderos de un inmueble

mortgage *n* hipoteca

mortgagee *n* acreedor hipotecario

mortgagor *n* deudor hipotecario

multi-family housing *n* unidad de viviendas multifamiliar

negative covenant *n* convenio negativo

notice to quit *n* aviso de desalojo

occupancy *n* ocupación, tenencia

open-end mortgage *n* préstamo hipotecario cuyo monto puede aumentarse

open-listing agreement *n* contrato no-exclusivo con múltiples agentes de bienes raíces

option to renew *n* opción de prorrogar

owner *n* propietario

partition *n* partición, mampara

party wall *n* pared medianera, pared común

permit *n* permiso, autorización

plat *n* solar, parcela, mapa

plottage *n* área de un solar

points *n* puntos

possession *n* posesión
premises *n* local, solar
prepayment clause *n* cláusula de prepago
principal residence *n* residencia principal
property *n* propiedad
property interest *n* derecho de propiedad
property taxes *n* impuesto sobre la propiedad
    inmobiliaria
proprietary lease *n* contrato de propiedad
purchase money mortgage *n* hipoteca que garantiza
    el pago del precio del bien hipotecado
quiet enjoyment *n* goce pacífico
quiet title *v* fijar la validez de un título de propiedad
quitclaim deed *n* acto de transferencia de un inmueble
    mediante el cual el otorgante renuncia a todos
    sus derechos de propiedad pero no garantiza que
    sus derechos sean superiores a los de posibles
    terceros
ratification *n* ratificación
real estate *n* bienes raíces, propiedad inmobiliaria
realtor *n* agente de bienes raíces, corredor de bienes
    raíces
realty *n* propiedad inmobiliaria
redeem *v* rescatar, redimir
redemption *n* rescate, redención
redlining *n* práctica discriminatoria mediante la cual
    se niegan créditos o hipotecas a ciertas personas
    según su origen étnico o su vecindario
referee's deed *n* escritura otorgada por árbitro judicial
rent *n* renta; *v* rentar
rent control *n* régimen de control de locaciones urbanas

Housing Law

Derecho de Vivienda

rent stabilization *n* estabilización de rentas
repossess *v* retomar posesión, readquirir posesión
residence *n* residencia
resident *adj/n* residente
residential *adj* residencial
residential market *n* mercado residencial
residential property *n* propiedad residencial
restrictive covenant *n* cláusula contractual mediante
    la que se limita la libertad de una de las partes
    de emprender ciertas actividades o de dar ciertos
    destinos a los bienes allí determinados
reversion *n* reversión de derechos al otorgante
revocation *n* revocación
rider *n* cláusula adicional
right of first refusal *n* opción de compra
right of survivorship *n* derecho de supervivencia
riparian rights *n* derechos del propietario ribereño
Rural Housing Service (RHS) *(Operates federal
    loan programs targeted to rural areas; makes
    direct loans and guarantees loans)* *n* Servicio
    de Vivienda Rural *(Gestiona programas de
    préstamos de vivienda rural)*
secondary mortgage *n* hipoteca secundaria
secondary mortgage market *n* mercado de hipotecas
    secundarias
security deposit *n* depósito de garantía
shelter *n* albergue
single-family home *n* vivienda unifamiliar
special use permit *n* permiso de uso especial
squatter *n* precarista, "paracaidista"

steering *n* práctica discriminatoria consistente en dirigir a ciertas personas hacia ciertas viviendas según su origen étnico

straight term mortgage *n* hipoteca que garantiza un pagaré con pagos periódicos de interés y pago íntegro de capital

sublease *n* sublocación, subarriendo

sublessee *n* sublocatario, subarrendatario

sublet *n* subarriendo, sublocación; *v* subarrendar

subsidized housing *n* vivienda con subsidio

subtenant *n* sublocatario, subarrendatario

tax deed *n* escritura a favor del adquiriente de un inmueble en una subasta destinada a satisfacer deudas impositivas

tax lien *n* privilegio (o derecho) preferencial a favor de los créditos impositivos

tenancy by the entirety *n* copropiedad entre marido y mujer sobre un inmueble de forma tal que al fallecer uno sus derechos pasan al otro, con duración común y similares derechos posesorios

tenancy in common *n* copropiedad de un inmueble de forma tal que al fallecer un copropietario sus derechos pasan a sus herederos y legatarios

tenant *n* inquilino, locatario

trespass *v* acción de entrar ilegalmente en un inmueble ajeno

uninhabitable *adj* inhabitable

utilities (*electric, water, heat, etc.*) *n* servicios urbanos (*electricidad, agua, calefacción, etc.*)

vacate premises *v* desocupar, ceder posesión

valuation *n* valoración, valuación, avalúo

Housing Law

wall *nm* pared

waste *n* deterioro de un inmueble, daño a un inmueble

wear and tear *n* desgaste y depreciación resultante del uso de un bien

wraparound mortgage *n* hipoteca adicional o secundaria otorgada para financiar la misma operación

zoning *n* regulación urbana, planeamiento urbano

IMMIGRATION LAW
DERECHO MIGRATORIO

Immigration law deals with the conditions under which **foreign** persons are admitted to the United States as temporary **visitors** or permanent **residents** and how they become U.S. **citizens**. These rules are now administered by the Department of Homeland Security.

Note: Numbers in parentheses refer to U.S. immigration forms.

A-1 visa *n* visa A-1
A-2 visa *n* visa A-2
A-3 visa *n* visa A-3
abused alien *n* extranjero víctima de malos tratos
abused immigrant spouse *n* cónyuge de inmigrante
    maltratada(o), víctima(o) de abuso
accompanying relative *n* familiar acompañante
accompanying visa *n* visa de acompañante
acquired citizenship *n* ciudadanía adquirida
adjust *(status)* *v* ajustar *(estado migratorio)*
adjustment of status *n* ajuste de estado migratorio
admission to country *n* admisión al país
advance parole *n* libertad condicional anticipada
advisal of rights *n* aviso o notificación de derechos
affidavit of support *n* declaración jurada de apoyo
    (económico)

affidavit of support (I-864) *n* declaración jurada de patrocinio económico

affidavit of support contract between sponsor and household member (I-864A) *n* contrato de declaración jurada de patrocinio económico entre el patrocinador y un miembro del hogar

affiliation *n* afiliación

affirmation *n* afirmación

affirmative asylum process *n* proceso de asilo afirmativo

agricultural worker *n* trabajador agrícola

alien *adj/n* extranjero

alien labor certification *n* certificación de trabajo a extranjeros

alien registration number *n* número de registro de extranjeros

alien registration receipt card *n* tarjeta de residente permanente

alternate chargeability *(rule under which an alien may be charged to a country other than the one of his/her birth)* *n* regla migratoria que permite bajo ciertas circunstancias atribuir a un extranjero como país de origen aquel de un familiar

alternate order of removal *n* orden reemplazante de traslado forzoso

annual limit *n* límite anual

Antiterrorism and Effective Death Penalty Act (AEDPA) *n* Ley de Antiterrorismo y Aplicación de la Pena de Muerte

applicant *n* solicitante

applicant for admission *n* solicitante de admisión

application *n* solicitud

application for adjustment of status *n* solicitud de cambio de clasificación

application for advance processing of orphan petition (I-600A) *n* solicitud de trámite por adelantado de la petición de orfandad

application for cancellation of removal *n* solicitud de cancelación del traslado

application for certification of citizenship (N-600) *n* solicitud de certificado de ciudadanía

application for employment authorization (I-765) *n* solicitud de autorización de empleo

application for replacement naturalization citizenship document (N-565) *n* solicitud de reemplazo del documento de ciudadanía por naturalización

application support center *n* centro de ayuda para solicitantes

application to register permanent residence or to adjust status (I-485) *n* solicitud para registrar la residencia permanente o para cambiar el estado legal

apply for a visa *v* solicitar visa

appointment package *n* paquete de cita

approval notice *n* aviso de aprobación

arrival category *n* categoría de llegada

arrival date *n* fecha de llegada

Arrival-Departure Card (I-94) *n* tarjeta de entrada-salida

arriving alien *n* extranjero que llega, entrante

asylee *n* asilado

asylee application *n* petición de asilo
asylee status *n* condición de asilado, estado de asilado
asylum *n* asilo
asylum officer *n* funcionario encargado de solicitudes de asilo
asylum seeker *n* solicitante de asilo
attestation *n* atestación
automated nationwide system for immigration review *n* sistema nacional automatizado para la revisión de inmigración
B-1 visa *n* visa B-1
B-1/B-2 visa *n* visa B1/B2
B-2 visa *n* visa B-2
bar to asylum *n* impedimento al asilo
bar to readmission *n* impedimento a la readmisión
battered *adj* golpeado *(m)*, golpeada *(f)*
battered child *n* niño golpeado *(m)*, niña golpeada *(f)*
battered spouse *n* cónyuge golpeada(o)
battered spouse waiver *n* exención para cónyuge golpeada(o)
battered spouse/child relief *n* reparación/ayuda/apoyo al cónyuge o infante golpeado/víctima de maltrato físico
biographical information *n* datos biográficos
Board of Immigration Appeals *n* Junta de Apelaciones de Inmigración
border crosser *n* cruzafronteras
border patrol *n* patrulla fronteriza
Border Patrol Sector *n* sector de la patrulla fronteriza
business non-immigrant *n* visitante de negocios no-inmigrante

cancellation of removal *n* anulación de traslado
cancellation without prejudice *n* anulación provisional
case number *n* número de caso, número de expediente
central address file *n* archivo central de direcciones
certificate of citizenship *n* certificado de ciudadanía
certificate of naturalization *n* certificado de
    naturalización
change of status *n* cambio de estado, cambio de
    condición
changed circumstances *n* circunstancias distintas
charge *(as to country of origin)* *n* atribución *(de país*
    de origen)
citizen *n* ciudadano
citizenship *n* ciudadanía
clear and convincing evidence *n* prueba clara y
    convincente
clear, convincing and unequivocal evidence *n*
    prueba inequívoca, clara y convincente
clearly and beyond a doubt *adj* claramente y más
    allá de toda duda
co-applicant *n* co-solicitante
conditional grant *n* otorgamiento condicional
conditional residence visa *n* visa de residencia
    condicional *(otorgada a cónyuge casado(a)*
    menos de dos años)
conditional resident *n* residente condicional
consular officer *n* funcionario consular
consulate *n* consulado
continuous physical presence *n* presencia física
    continuada
continuous residence *n* residencia continuada

Immigration Law

country of birth *n* país de nacimiento
crewman *n* tripulante
crew member *n* tripulante
criminal alien *n* extranjero delincuente
criminal removal *n* traslado por motivos penales
current *adj* actual, corriente
current status *n* estado actual, condición actual
custody redetermination hearing *n* audiencia para
      determinar la custodia nuevamente
cut-off date *n* fecha tope, fecha de vencimiento
danger to the community *n* peligro para la comunidad
defensive asylum process *n* proceso de asilo
      defensivo
deferred sentence *n* sentencia diferida, sentencia
      suspendida
Department of Homeland Security (DHS) *n*
      Departamento de Seguridad Nacional
Department of Labor (DOL) *n* Departamento del
      Trabajo
departure under safeguards *n* salida bajo
      supervisión de funcionarios migratorios
dependent *adj/n* dependiente
deport *v* deportar
deportable alien *n* extranjero sujeto a deportación
deportation *n* deportación
derivative beneficiary *n* beneficiario indirecto
derivative citizenship *n* ciudadanía indirecta
derivative status *n* condición indirecta, condición
      derivada
discretion *n* discreción
discretionary relief *n* reparación discrecional

Diversity Visa (DV) Lottery *n* Loteria Visas de Diversidad

documentarily qualified *adj* habiendo cumplido los requisitos documentales para una solicitud

domicile *n* domicilio

domiciled *adj* domiciliado

duration of status *n* duración del estado, duración del condición

economic persecution *n* persecución económica

eligibility *n* elegibilidad

emigrant *n* emigrante

employment authorization *n* autorización de empleo

employment eligibility verification (I-9) *n* verificación de derecho a empleo

English proficiency *n* dominio del inglés

entitled to be admitted *n* con derecho a ser admitido

establish eligibility as a refugee *v* establecer el derecho a la condición de refugiado

exceptional circumstances *n* circunstancias excepcionales

exchange alien *n* extranjero bajo programa e intercambio

exchange visitor *n* visitante bajo programa e intercambio

exclusion *n* exclusión

expedited hearing *n* audiencia sin demora

expedited removal proceeding *n* procedimiento de traslado expedito

expiration date *n* fecha de vencimiento

expulsion *n* expulsión

extension of stay *n* prórroga de estadía

Immigration Law

extreme cruelty *n* crueldad extrema
extreme hardship *n* privación extrema
Family First, Second, Third or Fourth Preference
     n Primera, Segunda, Tercera o Cuarta Preferencia
     (migratoria)
Family Unity Program *n* Programa de Unidad Familiar
Federal Poverty Guidelines *n* Pautas Federales
     Relativas a la Pobreza
Fiancé Visa *n* visa para novios con compromiso nupcial
filing fee *n* costo de tramitación
final order of removal *n* orden final de deportación
firmly resettled *n* firmemente restablecido
following to join *adj* próximo a convertirse en
     conviviente
forensic document laboratory *n* laboratorio forense
     de documentos
frivolous application *n* solicitud sin mérito
full-time student *n* estudiante a tiempo completo
gender-related persecution *n* persecución
     relacionada con el género
genuine fear of persecution *n* temor genuino de
     persecución
green card (I-551) *n* tarjeta de residente permanente
habeas corpus *n* habeas corpus
homeless *adj* sin hogar, sin techo
household income *n* ingreso del hogar
identification card *n* tarjeta de identificación
**Illegal Immigration Reform and Immigrant
     Responsibility Act** *n* Ley de Reforma a la
     Inmigración Ilegal y de Responsabilidad del
     Inmigrante

Derecho Migratorio

immediate family or relative *adj* familia o familiar
    inmediato
immigrant *n* inmigrante
immigrant petition *n* petición de inmigrante
immigrant visa *n* visa de inmigrante
immigration *adj* migratorio, inmigratorio; *n* inmigración
Immigration and Customs Enforcement (ICE) *n*
    Control de Inmigración y Aduanas
Immigration and Nationality Act (INA) *n* Ley de
    Inmigración y Nacionalidad
Immigration and Naturalization Service (INS) *n*
    Servicio de Inmigración y Naturalización
immigration attorney *n* abogado de inmigración
immigration hold *n* obstáculo de inmigración
immigration judge (IJ) *n* juez de inmigración
immigration lawyer *n* abogado de inmigración
immigration officer *n* agente de inmigración
immigration record *n* archivo de inmigración, informe
    de inmigración
inadmissible alien *n* extranjero inadmisible
ineligible *adj* inelegible
instruction package *n* paquete de instrucciones
interview *n* entrevista
intracompany transferee *n* persona trasladada por
    su compañía
joint sponsor *n* patrocinante conjunto
K-1 Visa *n* visa para novios con compromiso nupcial
labor certification *n* certificación laboral
Labor Condition Application (LCA) *n* Solicitud de
    Condición de Trabajo
last residence *n* última residencia

lawful permanent residence *n* residencia legal permanente

lawful permanent resident alien (LPRA) *n* extranjero residente permanente legal

lawfully admitted *adj* legalmente admitido

lay worker *n* trabajador lego

Legal Immigration Family Equity (LIFE) Act *n* Ley de Inmigración Legal y Equidad Familiar

legalized alien *n* extranjero legalizado

legitimated *adj* legitimado

level of education *n* nivel de educación

lottery *n* lotería

machine-readable passport (MRP) *n* pasaporte legible con máquina

machine-readable visa (MRV) *n* visa legible con máquina

maintenance of status and departure bond *n* caución relacionada con la conservación de la condición y la salida

mandatory detention *n* detención obligatoria

marital status *n* estado civil

marriage certificate *n* certificado de matrimonio

marriage fraud *n* fraude matrimonial

medical waiver *n* excepción por motivos médicos

migrant *adj/n* migrante

moral turpitude *n* vileza moral

motion for termination *n* petición de resolución

national interest *n* interés nacional

nationality *n* nacionalidad

naturalization *n* naturalización

naturalization application *n* solicitud de naturalización

naturalization ceremony *n* ceremonia de
   naturalización
naturalization court *n* tribunal de naturalización
naturalization papers *n* carta de naturalización
naturalized citizen *n* ciudadano naturalizado
negative factor *n* factor negativo
no-match letter (*letter from the Social Security
   Administration to an employer stating that an
   employee's reported Social Security number
   does not match SSA records and that employer
   must act to resolve the discrepancy or face
   possible penalties*) *n* carta de notificación
   de datos que no concuerdan (*carta de la
   Administración de Seguro Social a un patrón
   avisándole de una discrepancia entre el
   número de un empleado indicado por el patrón
   y el número contenido en los archivos del
   Seguro Social, y exigiendo que se resuelva
   tal discrepancia si se desea evitar eventuales
   penalidades*)
noncurrent *adj* ocasional, no recurrente
non-disclosure *n* no divulgación
non-immigrant temporary resident *n* no inmigrante
non-immigrant visa *n* visa de no inmigrante
North American Free Trade Agreement (NAFTA)
   n Acuerdo de Libre Comercio de las Américas
   (ALCA)
notice of asylum-only hearing *n* aviso de audiencia
   sólo para asilo
notice of consequences for failure to appear *n* aviso
   sobre las consecuencias de incomparecencia

Immigration Law

notice of consequences for failure to depart *n* aviso
sobre las consecuencias de no cumplir con la
orden de salida

**notice of consequences for failure to surrender to
the Immigration and Naturalization Service
for removal from the United States** *n* aviso
sobre las consecuencias de no entregarse al
Servicio de Inmigración y Naturalización para ser
trasladado fuera de los Estados Unidos

**notice of consequences for knowingly filing a
frivolous asylum application** *n* aviso sobre
las consecuencias de presentar a sabiendas una
solicitud de asilo sin mérito

notice of deportation hearing *n* aviso de audiencia de
deportación

**notice of intent to issue a final administrative
deportation order (Form I-851)** *n* aviso de
intención de expedir una orden administrativa
final de de deportación (Formulario I-851)

notice of intent to rescind *n* notificación de intención
de rescindir

**notice of intent to rescind and request for hearing
by alien** *n* aviso de intención de rescindir y
petición de audiencia del extranjero

notice of privilege of counsel *n* aviso del privilegio a
la asistencia de un abogado

notice of referral to immigration judge *n* aviso de
remisión a un juez de inmigración

notice of removal hearing *n* aviso de audiencia de
traslado forzoso

notice of review of claimed status *n* aviso de revisión de la condición reclamada

notice to alien detained for exclusion hearing (Form I-122) *n* aviso al extranjero detenido sobre una audiencia de exclusión (Formulario I-122)

notice to appear for removal proceedings *n* aviso de comparecencia por procedimiento de traslado forzoso

numerical limit *n* límite numérico

oath *n* juramento

occupation *n* profesión, empleo

Office of Immigration Litigation (OIL) *n* Oficina de Litigación de Inmigración

one-year rule *n* regla de un año, norma de un año

out of status *adj* fuera de estado legal, permanencia ilegal

overstay *n* estadía no autorizada

panel physician *n* médico del panel

parole *n* libertad condicional

parole board *n* junta de admisión condicional

parole someone into the U.S. *v* admitir a alguien condicionalmente en los EE UU

paroled alien *n* extranjero admitido condicionalmente

parolee *n* admitido condicionalmente

particularly serious crime *n* crimen particularment grave, delito particularmente grave

passport *n* pasaporte

per-country limit *n* límite por país

permanent resident *n* residente permanente

permanent resident card (PRC) (I-551) *n* tarjeta de residente permanente

petition *n* petición, solicitud

petition for alien fiance(e) (I-129F) *n* petición de un extranjero por compromiso matrimonial

petition for alien relative (I-130) *n* petición de un familiar extranjero

petition for review *n* petición de revisión, solicitud de revisión

petition to classify orphan as an immediate relative (I-600) *n* petición para clasificar a un huérfano como familiar inmediato

petitioner *n* solicitante

place of last entry *n* lugar de la última entrada, lugar del último ingreso

plausible in light of country conditions *n* creíble dadas las condiciones del país

political asylum *n* asilo político

port of entry *n* puerto de entrada

preclude *n* excluir, impedir

preference category *n* categoría de preferencia

preference immigrant *n* inmigrante de preferencia

Preference System *n* Sistema de Preferencia

pre-inspection *n* pre-inspección

prima facie eligibility *n* idoneidad prima facie

principal alien *n* extranjero principal

priority date *n* fecha de prioridad

public charge *n* persona indigente cuya manutención está a cargo del Estado

qualifying family relationship *n* relación familiar que confiere un derecho

quota *n* cuota

Real ID Act *n* Ley de Identificación Genuina

record of proceeding (ROP) *n* acta del procedimiento
records check *n* verificación de los archivos, inspección de los archivos
re-entry permission *n* permiso de regresar al país
refugee *n* refugiado
refugee approval *n* aprobación del estado de refugiado
refugee arrival *n* llegada del refugiado
refugee authorized admission *n* admisión autorizada de refugiado
refugee status *n* condición de refugiado, calidad de refugiado, estado de refugiado
regional office *n* oficina regional
registry date *n* fecha de registro
removable *n* sujeto a traslado forzoso
removal *n* traslado, traslado forzoso, repatriación, expulsión
removal hearing *n* audiencia de traslado forzoso
removal of inadmissible and deportable aliens *n* traslado de extranjeros deportables e inadmisibles
removal proceeding *n* procedimiento de traslado
removal process *n* proceso de traslado
remove *v* trasladar, expulsar, repatriar
remove at government expense *v* trasladar a expensas del gobierno
remove from a vessel or aircraft *v* hacer bajar a tierra de un barco o aeronave
renewal application *n* solicitud de renovación
request a visa *v* solicitar una/la visa
required departure *n* salida obligatoria
reserved decision *n* decisión reservada

Immigration Law

resettlement *n* reasentamiento

resident alien *n* extranjero residente

returning resident *n* residente en reingreso

safe haven *n* refugio seguro

safe harbor rule *n* estipulación en las leyes migratorias que ampara a un patrón que ha tratado de cumplir con la prohibición contra el empleo de extranjeros indocumentados

safe third country *n* tercer país seguro

sanctions for contemptuous conduct *n* sanciones por contumacia

service center *n* centro de servicio

significant possibility *n* posibilidad significativa

Social Security Number (SSN) *n* número de seguro social

special agricultural worker (SAW) *n* trabajador agrícola especial

special immigrant *n* inmigrante especial

special naturalization provisions *n* disposiciones especiales de naturalización

specialty occupation *n* profesión especializada

sponsor *n* patrocinador

sponsor's notice of change of address (I-865) *n* notificación del patrocinador sobre cambio de dirección

State Department response *n* respuesta del Departamento de Estado

stateless *adj* apátrida

status review *n* revisión de la condición

stowaway *n* polizón

student *n* estudiante

supplemental asylum application *n* solicitud de asilo
suplementaria

supporting document *n* documento justificante,
documento de respaldo

surrender for removal *v* presentarse para el traslado

swear in citizens *v* tomar el juramento de los que
adquieren la ciudadanía

swearing-in ceremony *n* ceremonia de juramento

swearing-in session *n* sesión de juramento

temporary protected status *n* condición protegida
provisional

temporary worker *n* trabajador temporal

terrorist activity *n* actividad terrorista

transit alien *n* extranjero en tránsito

Transit Without Visa (TWOV) *n* Tránsito sin Visa

transitional period custody rules *n* reglas de custodia
del período de transición

treaty investor visa *n* visa de inversionista para países
miembros del tratado

treaty trader visa *n* visa de comerciante de país
signatario del tratado

unaccompanied minor *n* menor no acompañado

United Nations Convention against Torture *n*
Convención de las Naciones Unidas Contra la
Tortura

unlawful stay *n* estadía no autorizada

unlawfully present *adj* presente ilegalmente

visa *n* visa

visa extension *n* extensión de visa

visa waiver pilot program *n* programa piloto de
exención de visa

Immigration Law

voluntary departure at the conclusion of proceedings *n* salida voluntaria al concluir el proceso

voluntary departure bond *n* caución de salida voluntaria

voluntary departure order *n* orden de salida voluntaria

voluntary departure prior to completion of proceedings *n* salida voluntaria previa a la conclusión del proceso

voluntary departure *n* salida voluntaria

voluntary removal *n* salida voluntaria

well-founded fear of persecution *n* temor fundado de persecución

withholding of deportation *n* aplazamiento de la deportación

withholding of removal *n* aplazamiento del traslado

TRAFFIC LAW
DERECHO DE TRÁNSITO

Traffic law deals with the rules governing the use of **motor vehicles** on public **highways**, the requirements for obtaining a **driver's license**, requirements concerning **insurance**, penalties for breaking traffic rules, and methods of enforcing **safety** measures such as **seat-belt** requirements and the ban against **driving while intoxicated**. In the United States, state law governs most traffic-law matters.

accident *n* accidente
accident report *n* informe de accidente
accumulation of points *n* acumulación de puntos
aggravated unlicensed operation (AUO) *n* manejo de
    vehículo sin licencia con circunstancias agravantes
aggressive driver program *n* programa para
    conductores de conducta agresiva
alcoholic beverage *n* bebida alcohólica
alternate-side parking *n* aparcamiento de lado
    alternativo, en sector alternativo
ambulance *n* ambulancia
answer a ticket *v* responder a una boleta de infracción
avenue *n* avenida
back-seat driver *(slang) n* pasajero entrometido
    que distrae al conductor intentando darle
    instrucciones

Blood Alcohol Concentration (BAC) *n* Concentración
de Alcohol en la Sangre (CAS)

brake *v* frenar

brakes *n* frenos

braking distance *n* distancia de frenado

breath test *n* prueba de aliento

bridge *n* puente

buckle up *v* abrocharse el cinturón de seguridad

careen *v* deslizarse (un vehículo) fuera de control

careless driving *n* conducción sin cuidado

Caution Precaución

cell phone law *n* ley que prohibe usar un teléfono
móvil al conducir

challenge a ticket *v* impugnar una boleta de infracción

child restraint law *n* ley que requiere que los niños
lleven cinturón de seguridad o usen asiento de
seguridad

child safety seat *n* asiento de seguridad

citation *n* emplazamiento *(orden de comparecencia
por una infracción)*

clean driving record *n* historial de conductor sin tacha

collision *n* colisión, choque

commercial motor vehicle (CMV) *n* vehículo
motorizado comercial

conditional license *n* licencia condicional

confiscated license *n* licencia confiscada

contest *v* impugnar

contributory negligence *n* negligencia contribuyente

corner *n* esquina

court appearance date *n* fecha de comparecencia en
tribunal

court appearance violation *n* infracción que requiere
    comparecencia
courtesy notice *n* aviso de infracción
crash *n* choque
Crossroad Cruce
crosswalk *n* cruce para peatones
curb *n* acera, bordillo, brocal
curve *n* curva
cut off *v* bloquearle el paso a alguien
Danger Peligro
Dangerous Curve Curva Peligrosa
Dead End No Hay Salida
default conviction *n* condena en rebeldía, condena
    por falta de comparecencia
defensive driving *n* conducción defensiva
Department of Motor Vehicles (DMV) *n* Departamento
    de Vehículos Motorizados
Department of Transportation (DOT) *n*
    Departamento de Transporte
designated driver *n* persona que no ha consumido
    bebidas alcohólicas y está designada como chofer
Detour Desvío
digital driver's license (DDL) *n* permiso de conducir
    digital
double parking *n* acto de estacionar en doble fila
drinking and driving offense *n* infracción de tránsito
    por conducir en estado de ebriedad
drinking driver program (DDP) *n* programa para
    conductores alcohólicos
driver *n* conductor, chofer

Traffic Law

driver improvement program *n* programa de
  mejoramiento para conductores
driver record *n* historial de conductor
driver's license *n* licencia de conducir, licencia
  de manejar
driving privilege *n* privilegio de conducir
driving school *n* escuela de manejo
driving through a safety zone *v* atravesar una zona
  de seguridad
**driving under the influence of alcohol or drugs
  (DUI)** *v* conducir bajo la influencia de alcohol o
  estupefacientes
driving while ability impaired (DWAI) *v* conducir
  con capacidad disminuída
driving while intoxicated (DWI) *v* conducir en
  estado de intoxicación
driving while license suspended *v* conducir con
  licencia suspendida
driving with an expired license *v* conducir con
  licencia vencida
drunk driving *n* manejar en estado de ebriedad
emergency brake *n* freno de emergencia
emergency stop *n* parada de emergencia
emergency vehicles *n* vehículos de emergencia
exceeding maximum speed limit *v* exceder la
  velocidad máxima permitida, rebasar la velocidad
  máxima permitida
expressway *n* autopista
failure to appear *n* falta de comparecencia
failure to obey a traffic control device *n*
  desobediencia de las señales de tráfico

failure to pay fine (FTP) *n* incumplimiento en el pago de multa

failure to stop at traffic light *n* infracción de no parar ante un semáforo

failure to use turn signals *n* infracción de dar vuelta sin señalar

failure to yield right of way *n* infracción por no ceder la prioridad de paso, infracción por no ceder el derecho de paso

failure to yield to pedestrian in crosswalk *n* infracción por no ceder la prioridad a un peaton en un cruce para peatones

fatal accident *n* accidente fatal

fatality *n* muerte

fault *n* falta, incumplimiento, culpa

Federal Motor Carrier Safety Administration (FMCSA) *n* Administración Federal de Seguridad de Vehículos de Transporte

fender-bender *(slang)* *n* accidente que causa solamente daño menor a vehículos

financial responsibility *n* responsabilidad financiera

fix-it ticket *n* infracción por mal estado del vehículo

flashing light *n* luz intermitente, luz relampagueante

flat tire *n* llanta desinflada, llanta ponchada, neumático desinflado

following distance *n* distancia que, por razones de seguridad, se guarda entre el vehículo propio y el vehículo delantero

following too closely *v* seguir el vehículo delantero demasiado cerca

freeway *n* autopista

Traffic Law

frontal impact *n* impacto frontal
front-seat occupants *n* ocupantes del asiento delantero
garage *n* garage, estacionamiento
gasoline *n* gasolina
gore zone/point *n* isleta canalizadora, zona de
    seguridad de entrada a la autopista
green light *n* luz verde
hazard *n* peligro
head-on collision *n* colisión frontal
hearing *n* vista, juicio
high-occupancy vehicle (HOV) lane *n* carril para
    vehículos de alta ocupación (VAO)
highway patrol *n* patrulla de carreteras
hit and run *adj/n* acto de atropellar y huir
honk *v* sonar el klaxon
horn *n* klaxon
impact *n* impacto
impede traffic *v* obstaculizar el tráfico
impound *(a vehicle)* *v* confiscar *(un vehículo)*
impounded vehicle *n* vehículo confiscado
improper *adj* inapropiado, incorrecto
improper passing *n* acto de pasar a otro vehículo
    incorrectamente
improper turn at traffic light *n* acto de dar vuelta
    incorrectamente ante un semáforo
in excess of *adv* excediendo, rebasando
infraction *n* infracción
injury *n* lesión
inspection sticker *n* calcomanía de inspección
insurance identification card *n* tarjeta de seguro,
    cédula de seguro

insurance settlement *n* arreglo de seguro, transacción de seguro

insurance violation *n* infracción de reglamentos relativos a seguros

interchange *(highway ~)* *n* encrucijada de autopista

intoxication *n* intoxicación

issuing officer *n* agente de tránsito que emite la infracción

jaywalk *v* cruzar la calle a pie imprudentemente

Keep Left Conserve Su Izquierda

Keep Right Conserve Su Derecha

lane violation *n* infracción relativa al uso de carriles

learner's permit *n* permiso de principiante

leaving the scene of an accident *v* abandonar el lugar de un accidente

left *adj* izquierda

liability insurance *n* seguro de responsabilidad personal

license plate *n* placa

loss of driving privileges *n* pérdida de privilegios de conductor

making unsafe lane changes *n* acto de cambiar de carril de manera imprudente

mandatory appearance violation *n* infracción que requiere comparecencia

mechanical violation *n* infracción relativa a la condición mecánica del vehículo

median strip *n* camellón, franja central

miles per hour (mph) *n* millas por hora

motor *n* motor

motorist *n* automovilista

Traffic Law

moving against traffic *v* conducir en sentido contrario al tráfico

moving violation *n* infracción de tránsito

National Traffic Safety Institute *n* Instituto Nacional de Seguridad de Tránsito

National Highway Traffic Safety Administration (NHTSA) *n* Administración Nacional de Seguridad de Tránsito

No Exit No Hay Salida

No Parking Prohibido Estacionar

No Standing Prohibido Parar *(en espera)*

No Stopping Prohibido Parar

no-fault state *n* estado cuya ley requiere de un seguro contra accidentes sobre la base de responsabilidad "sin falta"

non-mandatory appearance violations *n* infracción que no requiere comparecencia

non-moving violation *n* infracción no relacionada con la circulación

notice of suspension or revocation *n* aviso de suspensión o anulación del permiso de conducir

off-ramp *n* (rampa de) salida de autopista

one-way *adj* sentido único

on-ramp *n* (rampa de) entrada a la autopista

open container law *n* ley que prohibe tener bebidas alcohólicas abiertas al interior de un vehículo

overpass *n* paso a nivel

overtaking and passing *n* alcanzar y pasar a otro vehículo

overturn *v* volcar, voltear

paid parking permit *n* permiso de estacionamiento pagadero

parallel parking *n* estacionamiento en batería, estacionamiento en línea

parking lot *n* estacionamiento

parking meter *n* parquímetro

parking ticket *n* infracción por estacionamiento

parking violation *n* infracción por estacionamiento

passenger *n* pasajero

passing a stopped school bus *n* infracción de sobrepasar a un autobus escolar parado

passing on the right *n* infracción de pasar por la derecha a otro vehículo

passing on the shoulder *n* infracción de utilizar el borde para pasar a otro vehículo

pay by mail *n* pagar por correo

pedestrian *n* peaton

pedestrian crossing *n* cruce de peatones

Personal Injury Protection (PIP) *n* seguro contra lesiones personales

petty offense *n* falta menor

point *n* punto

point system *n* sistema de puntos

police report *n* informe policíaco, informe de policía

posted speed limit *n* límite de velocidad anunciado, límite de velocidad señalado

probationary driver program *n* programa para permiso de conducir condicional

proof of identity *n* prueba de identidad

proof of insurance *n* comprobante de seguro

property damage *n* daño material

Traffic Law

provisional driver's license *n* licencia de conducir
    provisional
pull over *v* acercar el vehículo a la orilla de la vía
    y parar
racial profiling *n* práctica policíaca consistente
    en atribuir sospechas a personas con ciertas
    características raciales
radar detector *n* aparato detector de radar
Railroad Ferrocarril
reaction distance *n* distancia de reacción
reaction time *n* tiempo de reacción
rear-end collision *n* colisión trasera
reckless driving *n* manejo imprudente, manejo temerario
red light *n* luz roja
reduce speed *v* reducir velocidad, moderar la velocidad
reduction in points *n* reducción de puntos
refusing to submit to a breath test *n* no someterse a
    una prueba de aliento
registration *n* matrícula
registration card *n* tarjeta de circulación vehicular
reinstatement *n* restablecimiento
respond *(to a ticket)* *v* responder *(a una infracción)*
rest area *n* área o parada de descanso
restoration *n* restablecimiento
restriction *n* restricción
revocation *n* revocación
right *adj* derecha
right of way *n* prioridad de paso, derecho de paso
road *n* carretera
road rage *(slang)* *n* el enfado extremo que siente un
    conductor con otro cuando éste conduce mal

road safety *n* seguridad vial

roadside *n* borde de la carretera, orilla de la carretera, lado de la carretera

roll over a vehicle *v* volcarse un vehiculo, voltearse un vehículo

rules of the road *n* reglas de tránsito

run a red light *v* pasar por alto un semáforo en rojo

run a stop sign *v* pasar por alto una señal de alto

safety responsibility hearing *n* audiencia sobre la capacidad de pago de un automovilista que ha estado involucrado en un accidente

Safety Responsibility Law *n* Ley de Responsabilidad y Seguridad

scene of an accident *n* escena de un accidente, lugar de un accidente

school bus *n* autobus escolar

School Zone Zona Escolar

scofflaw *n* persona que burla la ley

seatbelt *n* cinturón de seguridad

seatbelt law *n* ley sobre cinturones de seguridad

second offense *n* segunda infracción

sentence *n* pena

shoulder of the road *n* hombro de la carretera, borde de la carretera

shoulder harness *n* correa para el hombro, cinturon que sujeta el hombro

side collision *n* colisión lateral

sidewalk *n* acera

sign *n* rótulo, letrero

signal for help *v* hacer señas de auxilio

siren *n* sirena

Traffic Law

slide *v* deslizar

slow *adv* despacio

slow speed blocking traffic *n* obstaculizar el tráfico por lentitud

speed contest *n* carrera de velocidad

speed limit *n* límite de velocidad

speeding ticket *n* infracción por velocidad excesiva

stall on railroad tracks *v* quedar inmovilizado sobre una vía férrea

standing violation *n* infracción por detenerse en zona prohibida

state motor vehicle authority *n* autoridad estatal de vehículos motorizados

steering wheel *n* volante

Stop Alto

stop *v* parar, detenerse

stopping violation *n* infracción por parar en zona prohibida

street *n* calle

summary offense *n* infracción sumaria

suspension *n* suspensión

tailgate *v* no mantener su distancia, seguir demasiado cerca

thoroughfare *n* vía pública, calle transitada

through street *n* calle de vía libre

ticket *n* boleta de infracción

tinted window *n* ventana con láminas de protección solar

tire *n* llanta, neumático

tire blowout *n* reventón de llanta, reventón de neumático

toll *n* peaje

traffic *n* tráfico, tránsito
traffic court *n* tribunal de infracciones de tráfico/tránsito
traffic light *n* semáforo
traffic offense *n* infracción de tráfico, infracción de
    tránsito
traffic safety school *n* curso de seguridad vial
traffic sign *n* señal de tráfico, señal de tránsito
traffic ticket *n* infracción de tráfico, infracción de
    tránsito
traffic violations bureau *n* oficina de infracciones
    de tráfico
traffic violator school *n* escuela para infractores
    de tráfico
transmission *n* transmisión
turn *v* dar vuelta; *n* vuelta
turn in a license *v* entregar la licencia
unattended motor vehicle *n* vehículo desatendido
underage driver *n* conductor que no tiene la edad
    necesaria para conducir
under-insured motorist (UIM) *n* automovilista con
    seguro insuficiente
uninsured motorist (UM) *n* automovilista sin seguro
uninsured vehicle *n* vehículo sin seguro
unlawful use of median strip *n* uso ilegal de camellón
Vehicle and Traffic Law (VTL) *n* Ley de Vehículos y
    de Tránsito
vehicle code *n* código de tránsito
vehicle insurance *n* seguro para vehículo
vehicle registration *n* matrícula del vehículo
vehicular homicide *n* homicidio culposo por el
    conductor de un vehículo

Traffic Law

violation *n* infracción
violator *n* infractor
weave *(between lanes)* *v* culebrear *(entre carriles)*
wheel *n* rueda
whiplash *n* síndrome del latigazo, traumatismo del
    cuello
windshield *n* parabrisas
windshield wiper *n* limpiaparabrisas
yellow light *n* luz ámbar
yield *v* ceder el paso

Appendix 1 / Anexo 1

USEFUL PHRASES
FRASES UTILES

Stop!
¡Alto!

Stop or I'll shoot!
¡Alto o disparo!

I am a police officer!
¡Soy policía!

You are under arrest!
¡Queda arrestado!

Stand still and don't move!
¡Párese y no se mueva!

Put your hands behind your head!
¡Ponga las manos detrás de la cabeza!

Put your hands against *the car/the wall*!
¡Apoye las manos contra *el automóvil/la pared*!

Get out of the car!
¡Salga del automóvil!

Lie down on the floor (face down)!
¡Acuéstese en el piso (boca abajo)!

Drop the weapon on the ground!
¡Deje caer el arma al piso!

Don't shoot!
¡No dispare!

Exit the building!
¡Salga del edificio!

Come out with your hands up!
¡Salga con las manos arriba!

Open the door, I have a search warrant!
¡Abra la puerta, tengo orden de revisar!

Pull over and stop!
¡Mueva el vehículo hasta la orilla y pare!

Release that person!
¡Suelte a esa persona!

Fire!
¡Incendio!

Help!
¡Auxilio! / ¡Socorro!

Please tell me what happened.
Por favor, dígame que pasó.

I was robbed.
Me robaron.

Please repeat.
Repita, por favor.

Please speak more slowly.
Por favor, hable más despacio.

Do you speak English?
¿Habla inglés?

Do you understand me?
¿Me comprende?

What language do you speak?
¿Qué idioma habla?

What country are you from?
¿De qué país viene?

What is your name?
¿Cómo se llama?

Show me your *i.d.* / *driver's license* / *car registration* / *passport.*
Muéstreme su *identificación* / *licencia de manejar* / *matrícula de automóvil* / *pasaporte*.

I am going to give you first aid.
Le voy a dar primeros auxilios.

Cover this person with a blanket.
Cubra a esta persona con una cobija.

This woman is in labor.
Esta mujer está de parto.

Do not move this person.
No se debe mover a esta persona.

Are you choking?
¿Se está sofocando?

Is there a doctor here?
¿Hay un médico aquí?

Do you need a doctor?
¿Necesita un médico?

Are you hurt?
¿Está herido?

What hurts you?
¿Qué le duele?

Are you lost?
¿Está perdido?

Where do you live?
¿Dónde vive?

Where are your parents?
¿Dónde están tus padres?

Is there anyone (else) here?
¿Hay alguien (más) aquí?

Do you wish to make a statement?
¿Desea hacer una declaración?

You may make a telephone call.
Puede hacer una llamada telefónica.

You may call a lawyer.
Puede llamar a un abogado.

You may contact your consulate.
Puede comunicarse con su consulado.

Please come with me.
Por favor, venga conmigo.

Please wait here.
Por favor, espere aquí.

Please read this.
Por favor, lea esto.

Please sign this.
Por favor, firme esto.

Do you know how to *read/write*?
¿Sabe *leer/escribir*?

Please fill out this form.
Por favor, llene este formulario.

You are free to go.
Queda libre.

Thank you.
Gracias.

FRASES UTILES
USEFUL PHRASES

¡Alto!
Stop!

¡Alto o disparo!
Stop or I'll shoot!

¡Soy policía!
I am a police officer!

¡Queda arrestado!
You are under arrest!

¡Párese y no se mueva!
Stand still and don't move!

¡Ponga las manos detrás de la cabeza!
Put your hands behind your head!

¡Apoye las manos contra *el automóvil/la pared*!
Put your hands against *the car/the wall*!

¡Salga del automóvil!
Get out of the car!

¡Acuéstese en el piso (boca abajo)!
Lie down on the floor (face down)!

¡Deje caer el arma al piso!
Drop the weapon on the ground!

¡No dispare!
Don't shoot!

¡Salga del edificio!
Exit the building!

¡Salga con las manos arriba!
Come out with your hands up!

¡Abra la puerta, tengo orden de revisar!
Open the door, I have a search warrant!

¡Conduzca hasta la orilla y pare!
Pull over and stop!

¡Suelte a esa persona!
Release that person!

¡Incendio!
Fire!

¡Auxilio! / Socorro!
Help!

Por favor, dígame que pasó.
Please tell me what happened.

Me robaron.
I was robbed.

Repita por favor.
Please repeat.

Por favor, hable más despacio.
Please speak more slowly.

¿Habla inglés?
Do you speak English?

¿Me comprende?
Do you understand me?

¿Qué idioma habla?
What language do you speak?

¿De qué país viene?
What country are you from?

¿Cómo se llama?
What is your name?

Muéstreme su *identificación* / *licencia de manejar* / *matrícula de automóvil* / *pasaporte*.
Show me your *i.d.* / *driver's license* / *car registration* / *passport*.

Le voy a dar primeros auxilios.
I am going to give you first aid.

Cubra a esta persona con una cobija.
Cover this person with a blanket.

Esta mujer está de parto.
This woman is in labor.

No se debe mover a esta persona.
Do not move this person.

¿Se está sofocando?
Are you choking?

¿Hay un médico aquí?
Is there a doctor here?

¿Necesita un médico?
Do you need a doctor?

¿Está herido?
Are you hurt?

¿Qué le duele?
What hurts you?

¿Está perdido?
Are you lost?

¿Dónde vive?
Where do you live?

¿Dónde están tus padres?
Where are your parents?

¿Hay alguien (más) aquí?
Is there anyone (else) here?

¿Desea hacer una declaración?
Do you wish to make a statement?

Puede hacer una llamada telefónica.
You may make a telephone call.

Puede llamar a un abogado.
You may call a lawyer.

Puede comunicarse con su consulado.
You may contact your consulate.

Por favor, venga conmigo.
Please come with me.

Por favor, espere aquí.
Please wait here.

Por favor, lea esto.
Please read this.

Por favor, firme esto.
Please sign this.

¿Sabe *leer* / *escribir*?
Do you know how to *read* / *write*?

Por favor, llene este formulario.
Please fill out this form.

Queda libre.
You are free to go.

Gracias.
Thank you.

Appendix 2 / Anexo 2

MIRANDA WARNING
ADVERTENCIA SEGUN EL CASO MIRANDA

You have the right to remain silent. If you give up that right, anything you say can and will be used against you in a court of law. You have the right to an attorney and to have an attorney present during questioning. If you cannot afford an attorney, one will be provided to you at no cost. During any questioning, you may decide at any time to exercise these rights, not answer any questions or make any statements.

Usted tiene derecho a guardar silencio. Si renuncia a ese derecho, cualquier cosa que diga puede ser y será usada en su contra en un tribunal. Usted tiene derecho a llamar a un abogado y que lo asista durante el interrogatorio. Si no cuenta con los recursos para contratar a un abogado, se le asignará uno sin costo alguno para usted. Durante cualquier interrogatorio, usted puede, en cualquier momento, ejercer estos derechos, así como no contestar las preguntas que se le hagan o no hacer ninguna declaración.

About the Author

James Nolan, a consulting linguist and legal writer, has served as: Deputy Director of the Interpretation, Meetings and Publishing Division of the United Nations; Head of Linguistic and Conference Services of the International Tribunal for the Law of the Sea; Chief of the UN Verbatim Reporting Service; UN Senior Interpreter; and Linguist/Legal Writer with The Garden City Group. Holding both translation and law degrees, Mr. Nolan has taught in the interpreter training programs of the United Nations, Marymount Manhattan College, and New York University. He also conducts seminars in conference and court interpretation and is a consultant to the National Center for State Courts, the Canadian Forces Language School, and the Canadian Language Industries Association (AILIA). (Author contact: jamespnolan@aol.com)